# Life's Big Questions

# God's Big Answers

## by Brad Alles

# Table of Contents

# Acknowledgments

I would like to thank my editor at Concordia Publishing House for the opportunity to share some insights and information gained from over twenty years in the Lutheran high school religion classroom. I am also grateful to Paul Bahr, principal of Milwaukee Lutheran High School, and Rev. Bruce Harrmann, chairman of the Religion Department at MLHS, for encouraging me to put my thoughts on paper. For those who read or discussed sections of the book, I am especially thankful: Randy Weyhrich, Kevin Roach, Molly Gobeli, Andres Garuz, Brenda Mueller, Lauren Pankow, Dr. Angus Menuge, Dr. Gary Locklair, and Ward Alles. Your insight was greatly appreciated.

I wish to thank my parents for their never-ending love, support, and encouragement. My deepest thanks goes to my wife, Kelly, who always listens, understands, encourages, and advises. I love you very much. This book is dedicated to our daughters, Makiah and Kaleah. May you both find all your questions answered in Jesus, the way, the truth, and the life.

# Introduction

## The Reason for Life's Big Questions, God's Big Answers

According to a 2002 Barna poll, 70 percent of church youth left home after high school and then left the Church.[1] When asked the reason for leaving the Church, 32 percent (in an open-ended question) listed intellectual skepticism—religion made no sense, there was no proof, or there were no answers to legitimate questions (2005 National Study of Youth and Religion).[2] Young adults have questions—does the Church have answers?

Our culture redefined some terms that affect our youth and how they process God's Word. For example, 70 percent of church youth say no absolute moral truth exists, since truth is created by individuals and cultures.[3] Tolerance means recognizing that everyone's beliefs are equal—there is no truth greater than any other. Furthermore, no one has the right to judge anyone because claiming objective truth or judging the beliefs and lifestyles of others involves trying to dominate them.[4] Young people say there is no truth—is that true?

Josh McDowell notes that our young people's view of their church and youth groups is not positive. Besides church services, which are just events to observe with no relationships to people, youth find worship irrelevant to issues of today. Moreover, youth groups are often boring, with untrained volunteers and little content.[5] Youth say fellowship is irrelevant—does the Church have anything to say to us today?

Since our youth have questions about the veracity of their faith in a culture that says there is no truth, what are we doing to show them that Christianity is true and Jesus is real? How can we keep them in the one true faith? Hopefully, this resource will answer young people's questions and reveal truth that *is* relevant for us today.

I have been teaching religion in two Lutheran high schools for over twenty years. During that time, I have been invited to speak on various topics to youth and youth workers in fifteen states. Everywhere I go, people have the same basic questions. Young people want to study the Bible, but they also want to know it is true. What's more, they want to know how to apply Scripture to their lives. So back home I start every class, every day, with the same approach—are there any questions we should answer? I found that by explaining why Christianity is true and the Bible is dependable, students grow stronger in their faith. Here's an e-mail from Jackie, a 2008 graduate of Milwaukee Lutheran High School. After her first year of college, she wrote:

> I wanted to sincerely thank you for last year. I grew so much in my faith during my last two years at Milwaukee Lutheran. Your class did so much for me; I really don't know where I would be without it. It really makes me wonder how people without faith survive. You are one of the people of God that I respect most, and I wish that I could know the Bible like you do. Without your class I would not be able to answer half the questions that I have been faced with already this year. So I just wanted to say "thank you" for helping me grow.

By the power of the Holy Spirit, may we all grow in faith, and may this book shed light on the issues that trouble people in their search for the truth. May they find it in Jesus Christ, who is the way and the truth and the life (John 14:6).

# Chapter 1

## Are You Ready to Defend Your Faith?

If someone asked you why you were a Christian, what would you say? Would you say you're a Christian because you were raised that way, or would you say you're a Christian because you "just believe it"? Wouldn't that answer fit a person of another faith—perhaps a Muslim or a Hindu? When you give these responses to the question, you reveal a pretty weak rationale for believing Christianity. Do you have a good defense for why you believe what you do?

There is a better answer to the question of why you are a Christian. You are a Christian because Christianity is true. How can you defend that statement? That's the purpose of this book. So welcome to the wonderful world of *apologetics*.

Apologetics is, by definition, a defense of your actions or beliefs. It is explaining *why* you believe *what* you believe. We can find this concept in the Bible in 1 Peter 3:15–16.

> But in your hearts honor Christ the Lord as holy, always being prepared to make a defense to anyone who asks you for a reason for the hope that is in you; yet do it with gentleness and respect, having a good conscience, so that, when you are

> slandered, those who revile your good behavior in
> Christ may be put to shame.

We are always to be ready to gently and respectfully share the reason for the hope we have—why we believe in Jesus as the Savior who rescued us from our sinful condition and will grant us eternal life in heaven one day.

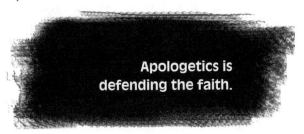

**Apologetics is defending the faith.**

As we defend our faith, explaining why we believe in Jesus as Savior, *what* we say is important—the content of our apologetics must be solid. We must know the facts and be armed with knowledge. However, that's just one part of the defense of our faith. The other part of the defense is *how* we say it—the delivery of those facts and knowledge. Peter instructed us to use "gentleness and respect" in explaining our hope that we have in Christ. Paul, by the inspiration of the Spirit, says a similar thing in 2 Timothy 2:24–26.

> And the Lord's servant must not be quarrelsome
> but kind to everyone, able to teach, patiently
> enduring evil, correcting his opponents with
> gentleness. God may perhaps grant them
> repentance leading to a knowledge of the truth,
> and they may come to their senses and escape
> from the snare of the devil, after being captured by
> him to do his will.

People need to hear the truth, and how you share that will make a big difference. Being a know-it-all or acting in a condescending manner is not appropriate—being kind in instructing others is what God calls us to do.

> **What we say (content) and how we say it (delivery) is important.**

Paul brings up another important aspect of apologetics. Remember that God saves people, not you. Yes, we need to know information and how to share it well—the "what and how" of apologetics. But our knowledge and instruction will not change anyone's sinful heart—only God the Holy Spirit can do that. He will convict the sinner of his or her condition through the Law and reveal the remedy for his or her sinful condition through the Gospel.

# Reasons People Reject Christ

Even as we share the Gospel and practice apologetics, some people may not believe what we have to say. In the book *The New Evidence That Demands a Verdict*, Josh McDowell explains.[6] Some will not believe since they are in a "snare of the devil, after being captured by him to do his will" (2 Timothy 2:26). Spiritual warfare is a real thing. When Jesus told the parable of the sower and the seed, He said some seed falls on paths and is eaten by birds before it can take root. Jesus explained what He meant in Luke 8:11–12:

> Now the parable is this: The seed is the word of God. The ones along the path are those who have heard; then the devil comes and takes away the word from their hearts, so that they may not believe and be saved.

You can defend the faith, handling both areas of content and delivery well, but some won't believe because they are under satanic attack.

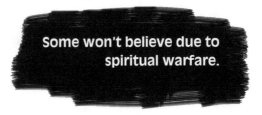

Some won't believe due to spiritual warfare.

Another reason some may not be converted to Christianity after you explain why you believe what you do is that people stubbornly refuse to admit they are wrong. Jesus faced a similar attitude in John 5:39–40. "You search the Scriptures because you think that in them you have eternal life; and it is they that bear witness about Me, yet you refuse to come to Me that you may have life." The religious leaders of Jesus' day would not come to Jesus, even though He fulfilled the Old Testament prophecies. In light of this prideful rejection of the truth, we can see why we are called to practice apologetics with "gentleness and respect." It will be easy to get mad at people, but that won't help your witness.

Some won't believe due to their prideful refusal to admit they're wrong!

A third reason some people reject faith is that becoming a Christian means leaving a lifestyle of sin. Jesus explained this in John 3:20 when He said, "For everyone who does wicked things hates the light and does not come to the light, lest his works should be exposed." You can say the right thing in the right way when defending the faith, but some will choose to stay in their sin rather than receive the Savior. They may feel that they're not *that* bad, or that they will convert later.

Some won't believe due to their unwillingness to change their lifestyle.

Knowing the three reasons why some reject the Christian message helps us diagnose why people aren't converted. We must realize that even if others reject faith, we did not waste our time because God's Word is effective.

> **For as the rain and the snow come down from heaven and do not return there but water the earth, making it bring forth and sprout, giving seed to the sower and bread to the eater, so shall My word be that goes out from My mouth; it shall not return to Me empty, but it shall accomplish that which I purpose, and shall succeed in the thing for which I sent it. Isaiah 55:10–11**

Furthermore, later someone else may add to what we shared, and ultimately the Holy Spirit changes people, as Paul said in 1 Corinthians 3:6–7: "I planted, Apollos watered, but God gave the growth. So neither he who plants nor he who waters is anything, but only God who gives the growth." Apologetics isn't easy, but it is definitely worth it!

# Chapter 2

## What Is a Worldview?

If you want to defend the Christian faith to anyone, whether a Muslim or an atheist, you need to understand that person's worldview. A worldview is a collection of the truth claims that explain the world and reality. It helps people make sense of the world; it is like a map they use to navigate through life.[7] Their worldview will tell them what is real and how to live, and it will answer basic questions.[8] For example, Christianity teaches that God exists, that faith in Jesus saves people from their sins, and stealing is wrong.

> **A worldview is a collection of the claims that explain reality.**

Technically, religions and philosophies have formal worldviews, and people adopt personal worldviews. Christianity and secular humanism, both dominant in the United States, have formal worldviews that explain reality and behavior and that answer questions people have. However, personal worldviews apply the broader view to a person's life. A personal worldview actually uses a formal worldview in an individual's life to make decisions. If a formal worldview is the map to navigate life, then a personal worldview involves actually using the map to go somewhere. Interestingly, people's formal and personal worldviews seldom match. In other words, people rarely use the map they own—they just leave it in the glove compartment.

To illustrate this idea, consider what Christianity says regarding Satan. The formal Christian worldview clearly states there is a natural and supernatural reality and an entity called the devil. However, George Barna in his book *Third Millennium Teens* showed that 65 percent of Christian youth don't personally believe in the devil.[9] Two-thirds of Christian teenagers reject this doctrinal aspect of the formal worldview and personally don't subscribe to it. Their personal and formal worldviews don't line up, and the inconsistency is obvious. But it's not just Christians who are inconsistent or hypocritical; most people fail to employ their formal worldview in their personal one, whether they are religious or not. For example, according to a 2007 Pew Forum on Religion and Life, 21 percent of atheists said they believed in God or a universal spirit![10]

> **Formal and personal worldviews seldom align, leading to hypocrisy and inconsistency.**

# Worldview Components

If a worldview is a collection of the truth claims that explain the world and reality, what are these specific claims? First, all worldviews begin with religious or philosophical assumptions—even if they claim not to.[11] If we do not grasp this fact, we miss a key witnessing opportunity when people share their worldview. Everyone has to start somewhere; the worldview "map" needs a beginning point, so assumptions are made. For example, atheism states there is no God. In contrast, Christianity states that God exists (theism), and He reveals Himself through His creation and His Word. Both start with a presupposition—there either is or isn't a God. A question to ask both would be "How do you know there is (or isn't) a God?" A Christian can reply there is a God since an orderly world exists, and moral order exists in this world. In other words, who, other than God, made everything working in precise order, as well as making humans with a sense of right and wrong? (We'll explore this defense in detail later.) On the other hand, when the atheist declares there is no God, how can he make such an absolute statement? Does he know everything? Has he traveled throughout the universe and now knows beyond a shadow of a doubt there is no supernatural realm?

How powerful is this starting point or presupposition to the worldview map? Some, such as Kansas State professor Dr. Scott Todd, won't acknowledge an intelligent designer because God doesn't fit their worldview.[12] In other words, "Don't confuse me with the facts; my mind is made up! There is no God." All worldviews have to start somewhere. What makes this point significant is that this assumption can carry you down very different paths of explaining life and how we should behave as we unfold each worldview map.

**All worldviews start with assumptions.**

Second, all worldviews have beliefs about reality and the source of everything.[13] Another term for this is a philosophy. Dr. Todd at Kansas State mentioned naturalism—the belief that reality is only comprised of matter, or natural things, with no supernatural realm. Everything that exists is just what we see in the world of nature; there are no spiritual forces or supernatural areas as well. If this world of matter is all there is, from where did it come? In his book and video series *Cosmos*, Carl Sagan basically says the cosmos is the only thing that will ever exist.[14] Do you see the assumption and the resulting explanation for all reality? All that ever existed in the past, exists now, and will exist is matter, and it assembled itself in clockwork precision. We'll discuss this concept in detail later when we address creation and evolution. However, understand this "no God" philosophy will have a tremendous impact on one's ethics, or beliefs, on how to live.

Now contrast Christianity's explanation of reality and the source of all things. God exists, and He is the source of all things, the natural and supernatural realms: "For by Him all things were created, in heaven and on earth, visible and invisible, whether thrones or dominions or rulers or authorities—all things were created through Him and for Him" (Colossians 1:16). Christians have an explanation for phenomena beyond the natural realm—God, miracles, angels, and demons. Atheism and secular humanism have no explanation for the supernatural since they assume it doesn't exist, and answers given to such phenomena will be lacking. This will be key in defending the faith and witnessing to others about God, since all people have to face the miraculous or unexplained in their lives. Some will say their map includes no supernatural realm, but that is not what they experience in life. Their worldview map and reality will not align, and you will be able to witness powerfully to them.

> **All worldviews tell us what's real and what is the source of all things.**

Third, all worldviews have beliefs about how to live.[15] Another term for this is *ethics*. Recall that according to atheism, no God exists. Furthermore, secular humanism believes that there is no supernatural realm—just this natural world in which we live. When it comes to answering questions on how we should behave, a final authority doesn't exist. Since there is no God, we each decide (or the government decides) what is good and bad. This is called *moral relativism*. The assumption that we're qualified to do this lies in the belief that man is basically good or neutral at worst, but not sinful as the Bible teaches. This view has huge implications. Consider Peter Singer, professor of bioethics at Princeton University and the issue of killing newborn babies, or infanticide. In his writings, Professor Singer declares that children younger than one month have no human consciousness and therefore do not have the same rights as others. As a result, the killing or starving of defective infants is not wrong.[16]

One cannot understate the importance of worldviews and their resulting ethical stands. A person doesn't just get up one morning and suddenly think it is okay to kill babies. The worldviews people are exposed to are comprised of ideas, and ideas have consequences.[17] Whether consciously or unconsciously, we are influenced by these worldview concepts. Such maps can literally lead us in deadly directions.

Christianity, on the other hand, leads us to life—eternal life in heaven through faith in Jesus' perfect life and sacrificial death for us. It also leads us in life—living in accordance with God's will. Christianity's ethical stance is moral absolutes: God has declared what is permissible and what is not according to His holy and perfect character. He knows what is best for us because He created us and reveals that in the Bible—like a carmaker gives you an owner's manual for your car. Returning to the map analogy, the Christian worldview will allow you to navigate through life best until you reach your destination, heaven. This is promised through Jesus, who is "the way, and the truth, and the life" (John 14:6).

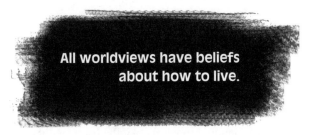

**All worldviews have beliefs about how to live.**

Fourth, all worldviews have to answer fundamental questions. These are questions all people ponder—issues universal to all humanity. Where did we come from? Why are we here? What can we do about evil and suffering? What happens when we die? Or stated another way, what are man's origin, purpose, and destiny?

Since everyone wants the answer to these basic issues, a worldview has to deliver solutions that make sense. But only Christianity gives a coherent set of meaningful answers.

To illustrate how other worldviews lack meaningful answers to life's big questions, take Dr. William Provine's statements in a debate with Dr. Phillip Johnson on creation and evolution. When relating the implications of evolution, Dr. Provine stated there were no gods, no life after death, no ultimate foundation for ethics, no ultimate meaning in life, and no free will.[18] Let those words sink in for a moment. Then consider how that worldview answers the issues of our purpose and destiny. It doesn't. There is no meaning in life. There is no life after death. The secular humanist map has gaping holes in it. People have legitimate questions that this worldview doesn't answer! On the other hand, Christianity can explain man's origin (creation), purpose (relationship with God and others), and destiny (heaven or hell) with information that can be intellectually and spiritually satisfying. And that leads us to evaluating worldviews—is this map any good?

> **All worldviews have to answer basic questions on origin, purpose, and destiny.**

# Evaluating Worldviews

People can believe whatever they want, but that doesn't make it true. I can believe I can fly, but when I fall off the roof instead of zooming through the sky, the truth (and the ground) smacks me in the face. So it is with worldviews. You can believe what you want—but is it true? The issue is not whether a belief is religious or scientific—the question is whether it is true.[19] Using the correspondence theory of truth—a philosophical belief that a statement is true if it corresponds to the facts of reality—let's set up some tests for worldviews.

The first test of a worldview is this: does it fit the facts, or is there any evidence to support it?[20] Truth is defined as "conformity to knowledge, fact, actuality, or logic."[21] When Christianity claims to be true, the proper question is "Are there any facts to back up the claims of the Christian religion?" Later we will see that there *are* historical, archaeological, and geographical facts to certify these claims as true. Consider again the map analogy: if I am reading my map correctly, and my map says turning right leads to my house, my house had better be there! The truth fits the facts, so a worldview has to fit the facts as well, since it claims to explain the world.

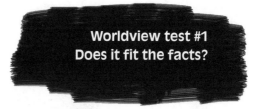

**Worldview test #1
Does it fit the facts?**

A second test for a worldview is that it doesn't have contradictions. If something is logically inconsistent, it cannot be true. Refer to the dictionary definition cited previously: truth is "conformity to knowledge, fact, actuality, or *logic*." For example, you can't be a married bachelor. Or take secular humanism's stance on ethics, or how to behave, which is moral relativism. Moral relativism says there are no absolutes. Notice the contradiction? To state there are no absolutes *is* an absolute statement! If you have contradictions throughout your worldview, it is much like a map that tells you that with one turn either to the left or the right, you will reach your house. Which one is it?

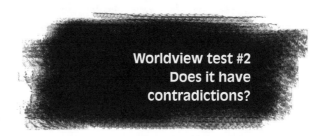

**Worldview test #2
Does it have
contradictions?**

A third test for a worldview is whether it is useful or relevant in life.[22] Recall that Dr. William Provine stated there were no gods, no life after death, no ultimate foundation for ethics, no ultimate meaning in life, and no free will.[23] Since these implications stem from evolution—the universe came about all by itself, without design or purpose—what is the benefit of following this worldview? Some may argue that because there's no God, we can live as we please. However, in reality, we can't all just live as we please. How do we decide what is right and wrong? If each person decides, what happens when one wants to steal and another says such behavior is wrong? If society decides what is right and wrong, what happens when one society disagrees with another? Would there be any moral justification for stopping another Adolf Hitler? We'll explore the ethical side of worldviews in depth later, but for now understand that if a worldview isn't helpful in life, it is like a map with huge holes in it.

**Worldview test #3
Is it useful in life?**

The following situations can lead to witnessing opportunities: exposing the disconnect between what people believe and what is actually true; displaying contradictions in beliefs; or revealing the irrelevance of worldviews. Your sharing of the Christian faith will be strongest when you show how it actually *does* fit the factual record, *does not* have contradictions, and *is* relevant in a person's everyday life, contrasted with the opposing worldview.[24] Knowing what to say regarding specific issues such as evolution is a perfect example. Did humans evolve? Or were humans created by God? What does the evidence say? Let's explore these questions in the next chapter and see where our maps lead us.

# Chapter 3

## Does Evolution Explain the World?

### The Theory's Assumption

Remember, all worldviews begin with assumptions and have to explain what is real so we can understand the world. Let's turn our attention to the issue of evolution and the origin of all things from a purely naturalistic viewpoint, without God, design, or purpose. The big bang theory states that billions of years ago, all the matter of the universe was compressed into a point. The point exploded, hence the term "big bang." The hot gases from the exploded point of matter went everywhere. Eventually, over billions of years, the gases cooled and formed the celestial bodies—stars, planets, and moons. That's how we got our universe. Any questions?

Well, evidently many Americans *do* have questions. According to a 2007 *Newsweek* poll, only 13 percent of Americans believe this theory. These are evolutionists in the sense that no God exists and had no hand in creation, while the same poll showed 30 percent of Americans believe God used evolution to create the universe. However, the biggest segment of the American public was the creationists—48 percent who believe God created everything in six days. (According to that poll, 9 percent of Americans don't know what to believe regarding life's origins.) What's going on here? We're inundated with evolution from television, movies, books, school, museums, and other aspects of life all the time, yet almost half of our country doesn't buy it.

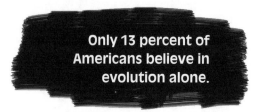

**Only 13 percent of Americans believe in evolution alone.**

I'll tell you why they don't buy it. It starts with an assumption. (Remember, every worldview starts with an assumption, even if it claims not to!) Carl Sagan believed only in the existence of the cosmos.[25] The 1933 Humanist Manifesto states the universe was already existing rather than created.[26] Evolutionists assume there is only a natural realm, with no supernatural realm. A simple question to ask is "How do you know this is true?" That's a powerful statement—how do you know there is only matter in the universe and not spirit also? Are you omniscient, or all-knowing?

Yet if you concede the point that matter making up the whole universe was always there, another question to ask would be "Where did it come from?" No one knows. Some say it came from a black hole. Some say it came from a mother universe. Where did those come from? No one knows. It is all one giant leap of faith, one large assumption, one starting point on the map. But the secular humanist will state that there is absolutely no God since He is not a part of the natural realm, but of the supernatural. Please remember this when people say Christians use blind faith but evolutionists use straight science. Everyone's map starts with a leap of faith—either God exists, or He doesn't. Are there both natural and supernatural areas on the map, or just a natural one?

But what's the biggest reason people don't buy into evolution? It fails worldview test number one—it doesn't fit the facts.

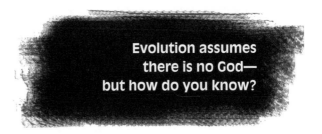

Evolution assumes
there is no God—
but how do you know?

# Questions for the
# Big Bang Theory

You don't have to be a genius to comprehend that basic scientific laws must be broken for the whole theory of evolution to work. (For a detailed discussion of all of these issues and more, please visit Answers in Genesis, the world's leading creation science organization, at answersingenesis.org.) As you recall, an explosion billions of years ago gave way to the universe working in clockwork precision. A question to ask regarding this big bang would be "What about the second law of thermodynamics?" This *law* (not a theory!) states that things in our universe go from a state of order to disorder, not from a state of disorder to order, unless acted upon by some outside, intelligent force. This law of decay, or "entropy," is used by creationists to argue against evolution, since everything we observe today is in opposition to the theory that an explosion gave rise to a perfectly functioning universe.[27] To drive your point home, ask what order came from the explosions at the World Trade Center in New York City when planes hit the twin towers and they collapsed? Did you see order from disorder, or just the opposite—chaos and destruction? If that is what happened with the demolition of two structures that worked perfectly, then how is it that an explosion of matter in space gave us a universe that functions with incredible accuracy and complexity all by itself? Here is your window of witnessing: the worldview map of what the evolutionist believes does not match reality—it doesn't fit the facts!

Although he supported evolution, let's listen to Albert Einstein himself, revered by evolutionists and creationists alike, discuss the issue.

I'm not an atheist, and I don't think I can call myself a pantheist (everything is God). We are in the position of a little child entering a huge library filled with books in many languages. The child knows someone must have written those books. It does not know how. It does not understand the languages in which they are written. The child dimly suspects a mysterious order in the arrangement of the books but doesn't know what it is. That, it seems to me, is the attitude of even the most intelligent human beings toward God. We see the universe marvelously arranged and obeying certain laws but only dimly understand these laws. Our limited minds grasp the mysterious force that moves the constellations.[28]

Cambridge University physicist, John Polkinghorne notes the incredible precision of the universe. From its smallest particles to the vast systems of space everything holds together and works. The very fact that this complex system exists at all implies that it has purpose.[29]

Scientists know the whole universe is incredibly finely tuned. But did the universe tune itself? How could lifeless matter, without intelligence, accomplish this? Or did someone, with life and intelligence, fine-tune it so we could live here? Sounds like God to me! That's why the article was entitled "Science Finds God," and why 48 percent of Americans believe God created the world in six days, just like the Bible says.

> An explosion couldn't bring about order due to the second law of thermodynamics.

# Questions for Life's Evolution

Now some will argue God didn't create the world like the Bible says, and He sure didn't create life here either—aliens did. I'm not kidding you. The theory is called "directed panspermia," and it states the first living cell must have come to earth from beyond our solar system. Remember there are no supernatural beings in the evolutionary worldview, so there must be a natural explanation for all things, even if it is from another planet. But think critically about this. How did these aliens evolve? From spontaneous generation, the theory that life came from lifeless matter? Life cannot come from lifeless matter due to the law of biogenesis, which states that life comes only from living things. Due to this law, there is no way chemicals in some soupy ocean three billion years ago formed life on planet Earth. This is why some folks actually believe alien life came here from another planet, and it gave rise to all life as we know it. When people propose this, please ask for proof (worldview test number one), and then ask how did aliens evolve from lifeless matter when the law of biogenesis doesn't allow that. What will be strange is how your faith in Jesus is belittled, and yet faith of a sort is exactly what is required to subscribe to this theory—faith in alien life.

Some scientists won't get into that science fiction stuff—they just admit their stubborn rejection of the Bible. Some scientists go as far as admitting that they don't want to believe in God, while at the same time admitting that they believe in life arising from lifeless matter, which they know is scientifically impossible.[30]

> Life could not have come from lifeless matter according to the law of biogenesis.

# Questions about Mutations

Many scientists go to great lengths to show evolution is true. We need to recall evolution is based on the premise that God doesn't exist, but the universe always did; it exploded all by itself and assembled itself without design, purpose, or God; and life came from lifeless matter. Remember these beliefs go against scientific laws, namely, the second law of thermodynamics and the law of biogenesis. So why stop now? If the theory of evolution is true, and scientific laws don't matter, then let's continue to show how life evolved from simple to complex organisms via mutations. But don't be surprised if the evidence doesn't support the theory, continuing to fail worldview test number one—does it fit the facts?

At the beginning of the film *X-Men*, Professor Charles Xavier says:

> **Mutation—it is the key to our evolution. It has enabled us to evolve from a single celled organism into the dominant species on the planet. This process is slow and normally takes thousands and thousands of years. But every few hundred millennia, evolution leaps forward.**[31]

Mutations work great in comic books and movies, enabling people to do all sorts of fantastic things—command metal like Magneto or heal like Wolverine. However, real life is another story. In evolution's story, one type of organism mutated and slowly changed into an entirely different organism over numerous generations—for example, fish mutated into reptiles, and reptiles into birds. This is called macroevolution.

The problem with this theory is that it has never been observed. We have never seen one organism mutate into another organism, except in comic books or movies. At Michigan State University, Professor Richard Lenski wanted to simulate evolution in real time. In his experiment, Lenski grew bacteria in his lab until he had the equivalent of a million years in human history. His conclusion: Essentially nothing new was produced. In the end, the bacteria were still bacteria.[32]

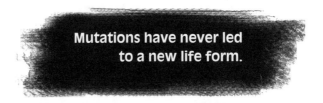

Mutations have never led
to a new life form.

Furthermore, the mutations observed in science are almost always harmful to the organism and are actually a loss of genetic information. In his book *Genetic Entropy and the Mystery of the Genome*, Cornell University Professor John Sanford concludes that most if not all mutations are detrimental.[33] Sorry, *Wolverine* fans—Logan can heal quickly due to his mutant abilities in *X-Men*, but no one in real life does. Contrary to what Professor X said at the beginning of *X-Men*, mutations are not the key to our evolution: no new organism has arisen from them, and they prove harmful, not helpful.

Mutations are almost
always harmful.

However, to show evolution is true, evidence is presented that reveals that mutations occur. For example, insects become resistant to certain pesticides. Since these bugs are bug-spray proof, this proves evolution. Not so fast—this is an example of microevolution, not macroevolution. Remember in macroevolution, one type of organism mutates and changes into an entirely different organism. The earlier example was fish changing into reptiles. But in microevolution, the organism remains the same, but with a small change within the species. These insects may now be resistant to a certain repellent, but they remain insects! There is a huge difference between these two types of evolution—micro and macro. Don't be fooled! One is scientific and observable (micro); the other is theoretical and unobserved (macro).

Then what do we see in museums, textbooks, and movies? Artists' renderings of what these half-fish, half-reptile creatures would look like. Just as in *X-Men*, imaginations soar as artists depict amazing new mutated creatures and life forms, all based in fantasy, not fact. There are no transitional forms alive today, or in the fossil record, that show macroevolution. Or maybe we should just listen to the late curator and paleontologist of London's Museum of Natural History, Colin Patterson, who had over seven million fossils at his disposal. He did not know of any evidence, "fossil or living," that provides a direct connection from one organism to another.[34]

> **There are no transitional fossils of one organism changing into another.**

The truth, by definition, fits the facts, so a worldview map has to fit the facts as well, since it claims to explain the world with the truth. However, we've seen just the opposite here in this brief overview of evolution. This map doesn't make sense: the universe exploded and arranged itself, and life came from lifeless matter, becoming more complex and mutating into different life forms. These beliefs go against scientific laws and evidence. If you want to learn more about these issues, visit Answers in Genesis, the world's leading creation science organization, at answersingenesis.org. The Christian worldview map makes more sense—it fits the facts of an orderly world that began perfectly, but is now disorderly due to mankind's sinful nature. Let's examine this map in the next chapter.

# Chapter 4

## Does Creation Explain the World?

### Arguments That God Exists

As we noted in chapter 2 on worldviews, everyone has to start somewhere. Our worldview "map" needs to have a starting point, so assumptions have to be made. Christianity states God exists, and He reveals Himself through His creation and His Word. A legitimate question to ask would be "How does one know there is a God?" We should have an answer. That's what apologetics is—defending the faith. Recall that Peter directs us to "always being prepared to make a defense to anyone who asks you for a reason for the hope that is in you" (1 Peter 3:15). So a Christian could reply there is a God since an orderly world exists, and moral order exists in this world. In other words, who, other than God, made everything working in precise order, as well as making humans with a sense of right and wrong?

All people can know that God exists. It is called the natural knowledge of God, and it comes from creation and our conscience. More specifically, cosmology, teleology, and moral order are the philosophical arguments for God's existence. What do those terms mean?

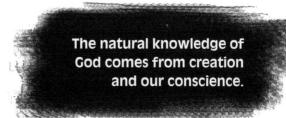

**The natural knowledge of God comes from creation and our conscience.**

Cosmology is the study of the universe's workings. Whatever begins to exist has a cause. The universe began. Since everything else we know has a beginning, who "began" the universe? God did. Genesis 1:1 says, "In the beginning, God created the heavens and the earth." The assumption is God was always there, or that He is eternal, and He created all things.

**Everything has a beginning. God created all things.**

Teleology is the study of design and purpose. Every design has a designer. A car or a laptop doesn't just appear out of nowhere— it is conceived in the mind of a designer and constructed out of materials. So it is with the universe and everything in it. All things are designed and constructed. John Polkinghorne, a professor at Cambridge University, recognized the order and structure to the universe and realized that the universe did not just happen, but there is design and purpose to its structure.[35] Who is the Designer? God is.

**Every design has a designer. God designed and created all things.**

These two concepts, cosmology and teleology, are important to remember. Everything has a beginning. Every design has a designer.

God designed and created all things. All people can know God exists. That's why Paul says, "For His invisible attributes, namely, His eternal power and divine nature, have been clearly perceived, ever since the creation of the world, in the things that have been made. So they are without excuse" (Romans 1:20).

What makes the Christian worldview map even more compelling is the fact that humans have moral order—a sense of right and wrong. Every moral law has a lawgiver. In the United States, we pay income tax on April 15. The law didn't appear out of thin air; Congress has the power to collect taxes according to section 8 of the Constitution. So it is with all of mankind; we all know there are certain things we should and should not do. These moral codes are universal; no matter where you go, people have these similar laws—don't lie, steal, kill, and the like. Since every law has a lawgiver, who gave these laws to all people? God did. Romans 2:14–15 speaks to this as Paul shows that Gentiles, who didn't have the Old Testament rules and regulations, still knew there were certain behaviors that were wrong.

> **For when Gentiles, who do not have the law, by nature do what the law requires, they are a law to themselves, even though they do not have the law. They show that the work of the law is written on their hearts, while their conscience also bears witness, and their conflicting thoughts accuse or even excuse them.**

Paul says the Law was "written on their hearts" so people knew right from wrong automatically.

**Every moral law has a lawgiver. God wrote the Law on people's hearts.**

If you recall, one of the problems associated with believing in evolution is the problem of the origin of life from lifelessness. The law of biogenesis rules this out—life can arise only from living organisms. Another question we could pose for the evolutionist would be this: How did consciousness develop, along with the moral code all humans have? Life had to come from lifeless matter (scientifically impossible), and this inanimate matter also had to think and develop a moral code of right and wrong. Do you see why so many people reject evolution? On the other hand, here's a map that makes sense. A designed, orderly world was made with moral order as well by God, a being who is perfect and all-powerful. That's what the Bible claims, and that's what we see today. It passes worldview test number one—it fits the facts.

Now that we have strong arguments for God's existence, other questions arise. Is God part of the universe, as pantheists believe? No. Genesis 1:1 clearly shows the difference between God and creation. "In the beginning, God created the heavens and the earth." Most Christians know this verse so well they fail to recognize how radical it is! God is not part of the world, as in other religions' creation accounts. He is not the freshwater god Apsu or the ocean and mother of all things Tiamat as in the Babylonian creation account. He created the water and everything else, so He is separate and transcendent from His creation.

As we look to the Bible for the answer to this question, we learn specifics about who God is—an all-powerful Creator, transcendent and apart from His creation, who puts His Holy Law in our hearts. This is called the revealed knowledge of God. From the Bible, we also learn that God is triune—three persons of Father, Son, and Holy Spirit, yet one God. We discover this holy being could not tolerate our rebellion, so He sent His Son to be the atoning sacrifice for our sins, demonstrating His unconditional love for us. Without Jesus' work on our behalf, we cannot enter God's holy presence when we die because of our sin. We will discuss these points in detail later, but these are aspects of the revealed knowledge of God, available only through the Bible. The natural knowledge of God, that He exists, is evident to all. Just look around. From where did this orderly universe come, working with clockwork precision? By chance? But just knowing some intelligent being is out there, who "wrote the books" in Einstein's library illustration isn't enough. We need to read the Book, the Bible, to hear the Law (that we have violated His holy will with our sinful lives) and the Gospel (that He forgives us through Jesus' perfect life and atoning death on the cross). This comes only from the revealed knowledge of God, through the Bible.

> The revealed knowledge of God (who He specifically is) comes from the Bible.

# Are the Six Days of Creation Literally "Days"?

Since we are using the revealed knowledge of God from the Bible to learn about man's origin, many other questions arise. One of these questions is "Are the six days of creation in Genesis literally 'days,' or are they long periods of time?"

To answer this question, look at the Hebrew word for "day" in the Genesis text, as well as the context for each of the six days of creation. You find the solution: the "days" are literally days, not long periods of time. The Hebrew word for "day" is *yom* and means a twenty-four-hour period, especially when you read the context of "evening and morning" for each of the six days of creation. James Barr, Hebrew professor at Oxford University, wrote,

> Probably, so far as I know, there is no professor of Hebrew or Old Testament at any world-class university who does not believe that the writer(s) of Genesis 1–11 intended to convey to their readers the ideas that:
>
> • creation took place in a series of six days which were the same as the days of 24 hours we now experience

- the figures contained in the Genesis genealogies provided by simple addition a chronology from the beginning of the world up to later stages in the biblical story

- Noah's flood was understood to be world-wide and extinguish all human and animal life except for those in the ark.[36]

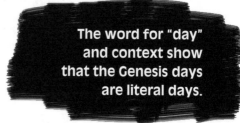

The word for "day" and context show that the Genesis days are literal days.

Furthermore, other parts of the Bible refer to a six-day creation account. For example, Exodus 20:9–11:

> Six days you shall labor, and do all your work, but the seventh day is a Sabbath to the LORD your God. . . . For in six days the LORD made heaven and earth, the sea, and all that is in them, and rested on the seventh day. Therefore the LORD blessed the Sabbath day and made it holy.

That's pretty clear, isn't it?

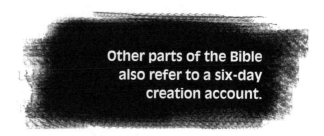

Other parts of the Bible also refer to a six-day creation account.

# How Old Is the Earth?

Professor Barr mentioned the Genesis genealogies providing a history of man by simple addition. If you read chapters 5 and 11 of Genesis and literally "do the math," you can get a sense of the earth's age—approximately six thousand years old. Moreover, using a wide variety of sources, from outer space to planet Earth, by measuring things such as the remnants of supernovas, or monitoring the growth of coral reefs, scientists verify that the earth is merely thousands of years old.

Scientist tell us that our universe experiences one supernova, or exploding star every twenty-five years. The remaining dust clouds (i.e., Crab Nebula) from these supervovas could remain visible for a million years. In actual observation scientists can identify only about 200 of these massive dust clouds. Simple calculations show that this is only consistent with about 7,000 years of supernovas, not the billions claimed by some observers.[37]

Or take coral reefs as another example. The Eniwetok Atoll in the Marshall Islands has the thickest known reef on the planet. At the highest known growth rates, it would have taken just 3,240 years to grow this large, not hundreds of thousands or more as some argue.[38] The worldview test of fitting the facts is met once again. This worldview map, where the earth is thousands of years old, was common until the 1800s, when evolutionists taught the earth was millions of years old. On what did they base this claim? The assumption that evolution was true, and there was no supernatural realm.

**According to the Bible, the earth is about six thousand years old.**

Today, evolutionists state the universe started with the big bang about 14 billion years ago, making the earth about 4.5 billion years old. Since radiometric dating methods are used to measure the earth's age in rocks and other artifacts, we need to know these dating methods are based on some assumptions as well. These assumptions include the following: (1) it's possible to know the initial amount of the element to be measured; (2) nothing has contaminated the element; and (3) the decay rate has remained constant. For example, potassium–argon is supposedly one of the most reliable radiometric dating methods. Yet rocks formed from volcanoes that erupted on known dates in history have been radiometrically measured with potassium–argon and dated from 1.7 to 15.3 million years old! Not only is this a huge range of years, but they are also all wrong since we know the exact date these rocks were formed from volcanic lava! Which worldview map doesn't fit the facts? Engineer and author Bodie Hodge said:

> If radiometric dating fails to get an accurate date on something of which we *do* know the true age, then how can it be trusted to give us the correct age for rocks that had no human observers to record when they formed? It is far more rational to trust the Word of the God who created the world, knows its history perfectly, and has revealed sufficient information in the Bible for us to understand that history and the age of the creation.[39]

**Radiometric dating fails to get correct dates on things which we do know the true age.**

# The Genesis Account of Creation and Jesus

Continuing to follow the literal Genesis account of creation, which is what Professor Barr said the text is intending to convey, the sequence of days and their created elements are as follows.

- On day 1, God made a watery, formless mass along with light, but this light was not the sun (more about this later).

- On day 2, God formed the earth entirely out of the water and added an atmosphere that separated either clouds or a possible extra layer of water vapor above this watery planet. Some creationists believe this extra atmospheric layer would provide certain benefits to life on the planet. It would create a greenhouse effect for a warmer climate all over and block harmful radiation for longer life.[40] This would explain why people in the Genesis genealogies lived so long before the flood—the environment was much different (and better!) than it is today.

- On day 3, God made land and plants.

- On day 4, God made the sun, moon, and the stars. Recall on day 1, God created light. It was not the sun; the Hebrew word is simply "light." What was this light? No one knows. But on day 4, God made the sun. Notice how God created the sun after the plants had already been created on day 3. Why? Perhaps it was to show that God, not the sun, gives life. Many cultures later worshiped the sun and have a "sun-god"; however, God, not the sun, gives life.

- On day 5, God made fish and birds.

- Finally, on day 6, God made land animals as well as Adam and Eve. In Genesis 1:26, the triune God, Father, Son, and Holy Spirit, spoke when "They" said, "Let *Us* make man in *Our* image, after *Our* likeness" (emphasis added). The phrase the "image and likeness of God" means Adam and Eve were made righteous and holy. They were made in God's spiritual image, not physical appearance, since God is spirit as Jesus reminds us in John 4:24.

- On the seventh day, God rested from His creative work. The word doesn't mean He was tired; He was just finished! He also made it holy and proclaimed later that Israel should not work on the Sabbath, because "In six days the LORD made heaven and earth, and on the seventh day He rested and was refreshed" (Exodus 31:17). (Yet another verse speaks to a literal six-day creation.)

Often skeptics of the Bible try to point out apparent contradictions in the first two chapters of Genesis—two seemingly separate creation accounts. But these are not two accounts; Genesis 1:1–2:3 simply provides a general overview of everything that happened on days 1 through 7. Then Genesis 2:4–25 gives a more detailed account of man's creation on day 6. Why is this detailed account given? Because man is the crowning element of God's creation, and God has a special relationship with mankind.

Even the word for God reveals this special relationship. Moses uses the Hebrew word *Elohim*, a general term for God in Genesis 1:1–2:3. But in Genesis 2:4–25, Moses uses *Yahweh* (literally "I AM"), the covenant name for God, revealing a more personal side of the Creator.

As God creates Adam on day 6, just three days after making all the plants, God also creates a garden for man. Now Adam hadn't seen God do anything on days 1 through 5 because he was not around, so before any plant grew from seed, God makes a garden especially for Adam and Eve as proof of His creative ability.

Appropriately, the name Adam means "man." When no suitable helper is found for Adam, God provides Eve. Eve means "living," for she would be "the mother of all living" (Genesis 3:20). We have all descended from these two people. All of us are related in one race—the human race. Jesus confessed this in Mark 10:6, "But from the beginning of creation, 'God made them male and female.'" Jesus' own words support the literal six-day creation account—they should, because He was there! John 1:1–3 reminds us:

> In the beginning was the Word, and the Word was with God, and the Word was God. He was in the beginning with God. All things were made through Him, and without Him was not any thing made that was made.

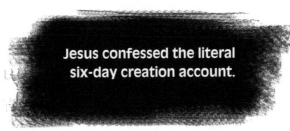

**Jesus confessed the literal six-day creation account.**

In the final analysis, we are left with two distinct worldviews—creation and evolution—yet only one world. We all live on this one planet, yet here are two vastly different ways to interpret what we see. Which map is correct? Research chemist and author Jonathan Sarfati wrote,

> Many people have the false belief that "science" has proven the earth to be billions of years old, and that every living thing descended from a single cell which itself is the result of chance combination of chemicals. However, science deals with repeatable observations in the present, while evolution/long age ideas are based on assumptions from outside science about the unobservable past. Facts do not speak for themselves—they must be interpreted according to a framework. It is not a case of religion/creation/subjectivity vs. science/evolution/objectivity. Rather, it is the biases of the religions of Christianity and of humanism interpreting the same facts in diametrically opposite ways.[41]

And following these worldview maps will lead us down dramatically different roads when it comes to the next aspect of a worldview—resulting ethical systems. A worldview not only tells you what is real (a natural realm alone, or a natural and supernatural together), but it also tells you how to live. Is man basically good? Or is man sinful? If man is sinful, how did evil enter the world? What can we do about it? Let's continue to unfold these maps and see what develops.

# Chapter 5

## What Are Humans?
### Our True Purpose

What are you? Are you a unique creation of a loving God or a random collection of molecules? If you consider yourself from the viewpoint of creation or evolution, you will come out with very different perspectives. The meaning of anything comes from its origin; to understand it, you must grasp the origin. For instance, Spider-Man's origin is vital to understanding what compels him to be a superhero: "with great power comes great responsibility." Likewise, our meaning stems from our origin. To understand ourselves, we must grasp whether we are divinely created or random accidents. Remember that the worldview tells you what is philosophically real, so if evolution is true, and no God exists, you are no more than an accident. This is stated bluntly in the comic book and film *Watchmen* by Alan Moore. "Life's so fragile, a successful virus clinging to a speck of mud suspended in endless nothing. . . . The horror is this: in the end, it is simply a picture of empty, meaningless, blackness. We are alone. There is nothing else."[42]

Now *that* is being brutally honest about what we are if the worldview of secular humanism and evolution is correct. It isn't pretty, but it is exactly what Dr. Provine stated in his debate with Dr. Johnson regarding the philosophical implications of evolution. As stated earlier in the book, Provine said if evolution was true, then there were no gods, no life after death, no ultimate foundation for ethics, no free will, and *no ultimate meaning in life*. How do you like *them* apples?

> **One implication of evolution is we have no purpose and no meaning in life.**

Yet purpose in life is one of the key elements all people seek. We all wonder, "Why am I here? What is my purpose in life?" This fundamental question is one all worldviews have to answer, yet it is woefully absent here. Is it any wonder that people today have turned to anything that will give some reason to continue—some purpose to find meaning in life? Some turn to relationships, some to money, some to escapism in drugs and alcohol. Yet many are still unfulfilled. Why is this?

The reason people are unfulfilled is they don't understand they were created to have a relationship with God that only He can satisfy. He created us because He loves us; "God is love" (1 John 4:8). Just as parents have children because they love them, so God "had" us because He loves us. God also created us for a purpose. Genesis 1:31 tells us God made Adam and Eve and saw they were "very good." We are not accidents. Revelation 4:11 adds, "You created all things, and by Your will they existed and were created."

> **God created us because He loves us and has a purpose for us.**

So if God loves us and created us on purpose, what were we supposed to do? Genesis 1:28 says,

> **And God blessed them. And God said to them, "Be fruitful and multiply and fill the earth and subdue it and have dominion over the fish of the sea and over the birds of the heavens and over every living thing that moves on the earth."**

God told Adam and Eve they had two purposes. The first was to "be fruitful and multiply." But God wasn't talking math equations; He wanted them to have children. Here at the very beginning of Scripture we see the foundation for marriage and family today. The second purpose was to "fill the earth and subdue it." In other words, they were to build societies and civilizations. This serves as foundation for everything else we do today; whether farming, business, education, or whatever.

These two purposes of filling the earth with families and subduing it with civilizations are done daily when we get married, start families, begin jobs, start new companies, and invent new devices. Author and teacher Nancy Pearcey points out that although these things are common to all people, they reveal our true nature, the way God created us to function.[43] Even after Christ came to earth to save us, we are still called to honor God on earth in whatever we do. Paul says, "So, whether you eat or drink, or whatever you do, do all to the glory of God" (1 Corinthians 10:31) and "Whatever you do, work heartily, as for the Lord and not for men" (Colossians 3:23). If you have ever noticed why you get bored, you may come to realize that you were made to do something. That's because God made you to work—but not in a negative sense. Work is *not* a bad thing; remember, Adam was made to take care of the garden as a job *before* the fall into sin: "The Lord God took the man and put him in the garden of Eden to work it and keep it" (Genesis 2:15).

After the fall, however, work was hard, and man would eat by the sweat of his brow. But work in and of itself is not bad. How wonderful to know you are loved by God, made with this purpose: to bring honor and glory to Him in all you do and by being creative with the talents and gifts He has given you. In this way, we continue to reflect God's creative nature, which started in the first six days of creation. God's children are acting like their heavenly Father!

> **Our purpose is to glorify God through using our talents and gifts in all we do.**

Earlier we addressed the tests for worldviews: if a worldview isn't helpful in life, it is like a map with huge holes in it. This third test is on display here. Secular humanism and evolution give us no purpose for life, yet Christianity does. The Christian map is helpful and relevant for navigating through life—there is purpose and meaning to our existence and all we do! Nancy Pearcey said it best in her book *Total Truth*:

> No one can live without a sense of purpose or direction, a sense that his or her life has significance as part of a cosmic story . . . but at some point, these temporal things (earning a degree, getting a job) fail to fulfill the deeper hunger for eternity in the human spirit. . . . Our hearts are restless . . . until we find our rest in Him.[44]

## Our True Nature

So if mankind's purpose is to glorify God through using our talents and gifts in all we do, is a murderer glorifying God? Of course not! When God made Adam and Eve, they were deemed "very good," along with all creation. Yet that's not exactly how you would describe the world today! What happened? To understand our planet, we need to realize the nature of humans. Our true nature is not good or basically neutral, as people in worldviews other than Christianity contend. Just look around. Do you lock your doors at night? That should tell you immediately our true nature—sinful.

The fall into sin was mentioned earlier. The change in human nature from very good to sinful occurred when Adam and Eve disobeyed God and ate from the tree of the knowledge of good and evil, a tree they were prohibited from eating because it would lead to their death (Genesis 3:1–7). Why would Adam and Eve eat from a tree they were told to avoid? Because they exercised their free will and chose to go against God's expressed will.

God gave Adam and Eve the dignity of free will. They could choose to obey God or not. Genesis 2:16–17 says, "And the LORD God commanded the man, saying, 'You may surely eat of every tree of the garden, but of the tree of the knowledge of good and evil you shall not eat, for in the day that you eat of it you shall surely die.' " Some ask, "If God knows everything, or is omniscient, didn't He know Adam and Eve would eat from the forbidden tree and ruin a perfect world?" The answer: "Yes, He did know." Then people ask, "Why would He allow that? Why not stop them?" The answer to that question goes back to the dignity of free will.

Consider God's options in creation. Because He knows humans will sin and ruin everything, He could have (1) created nothing; (2) created humans without free will, making them robots; (3) created humans with free will and destroyed them when they disobeyed; or (4) created humans with free will and offered forgiveness when they disobeyed. Since the Bible is clear that "God is love," options 1, 2, and 3 don't seem to fit. If God is loving and creative, would He do nothing? That runs counter to His very nature! If God is loving and creative, would He make us robots so we don't disobey? What kind of relationship is that? Is the movie *The Stepford Wives* an illustration of the kind of relationship we want when we're married—a robot spouse? If God is loving and creative, would He give us free will, yet destroy us when we sin? Where is the love and mercy? That's why option 4, free will given to humans, along with mercy and grace in Jesus Christ for our disobedience, is the option that fits a loving and creative God.

> Our true nature is not good but sinful, because Adam and Eve rebelled against God's Law.

# The Source of Evil

It is interesting to listen to other people's explanation of the source of evil in the world today. The Romantics claimed society corrupted innocent children. Darwinian evolutionists saw murder as a remnant from our "survival of the fittest" past. Sigmund Freud believed problems were due to our repressed sexual desires. Karl Marx thought suffering was from the oppressive ruling class. Evolutionary biologists believe our human behavior is driven by our genes' desire to replicate. Prison Fellowship founder Charles Colson explains what all these theories have in common: "They all treat human responsibility as an illusion. The underlying reason for this is their dismissal of God. Because they get God wrong, they also misunderstand human nature."[45]

But there's another reason Adam and Eve rebelled against God. They not only exercised their free will, but they were also tempted by Satan in the form of a serpent. Recall that the Christian worldview includes natural and supernatural realms. Whereas the evolutionist has no supernatural realm and no room for angels and demons, Christianity can explain why cultures all over the world believe in spirits, or why today the Roman Catholic Church (and other denominations) performs exorcisms and deliverance ministry on demon-possessed people. The Roman Catholic Church's New York archdiocese investigates about forty cases per year and performs exorcisms in about 10 percent of the cases after ruling out physical or psychological problems.[46] If there's no supernatural realm of the demonic, what is going on here?

Satan originally was created perfect and served God as an angel until he rebelled in pride, as recorded in Ezekiel 28:14–17. (Some Bible commentators believe that this prophecy uses Satan's prideful fall from heaven as a comparison to an arrogant king on earth.)

You were an anointed guardian cherub. I placed you; you were on the holy mountain of God; in the midst of the stones of fire you walked. You were blameless in your ways from the day you were created, till unrighteousness was found in you. In the abundance of your trade you were filled with violence in your midst, and you sinned; so I cast you as a profane thing from the mountain of God, and I destroyed you, O guardian cherub, from the midst of the stones of fire. Your heart was proud because of your beauty; you corrupted your wisdom for the sake of your splendor. I cast you to the ground; I exposed you before kings, to feast their eyes on you.

Here is the origin of the devil, the tempter of Adam and Eve. Satan rebelled against a holy God because "unrighteousness was found" in him, namely, violence and pride. It sounds like this angel didn't want to follow God but rather do his own thing. This is the source of evil in the world. When the first two people listened to Satan's lies—they wouldn't die if they ate from the forbidden tree, rather they would be like God—Adam and Eve brought sin and rebellion into an otherwise perfect and very good world. They thought they could do their own thing. They were wrong, and the world has suffered ever since. God cursed the serpent, cursed the ground Adam had to work to produce food, thus making labor hard, and increased Eve's pains in childbearing (Genesis 3:8–19). Ultimately, because they disobeyed, mankind would not live forever, but would die.

> **The world's source of evil is Satan, an angel who didn't obey God but tempted man to sin.**

If we fail to grasp the significance, in the Christian worldview, not only of the creation, but also of the fall, we fail to understand the world around us. During our examination of creation, we discussed how orderly the universe is. You may have thought to yourself, Wait a minute. The world is orderly, but not perfect. Exactly! There are disasters, droughts, disease, and worst of all, death. The Christian worldview explains how the world came into existence and why it isn't in perfect condition. This map matches the world we see on a daily basis. Our sinful human nature led to a corrupted earthly existence, full of suffering and sin. So what can we do about it? Or better yet, what has God done about it?

# The Solution to Evil

Remember what Nancy Pearcey said: "At some point, these temporal things (earning a degree, getting a job) fail to fulfill the deeper hunger for eternity in the human spirit. . . . Our hearts are restless . . . until we find our rest in Him."[47] While it is true that we were made to be creative and do something with our God-given abilities, all the achievements we make fail to satisfy a spiritual need within us. When sin entered the world, death entered the world, as God said, "For in the day that you eat of it you shall surely die" (Genesis 2:17). Mankind's greatest need was not more food, possessions, or achievements, but life—eternal life only God could grant! To cover Adam and Eve's nakedness, God killed an animal and made clothes for them as recorded in Genesis 3:21: "And the LORD God made for Adam and for his wife garments of skins and clothed them." But to cover our sinfulness, God killed His Son, Jesus, and made "clothes" for us as recorded in Isaiah 61:10:

> I will greatly rejoice in the LORD; my soul shall
> exult in my God, for He has clothed me with the
> garments of salvation; He has covered me with
> the robe of righteousness, as a bridegroom decks
> himself like a priest with a beautiful headdress,
> and as a bride adorns herself with her jewels.

By trusting in Jesus' perfect life and sacrificial death, we are covered with "garments of salvation . . . the robe of righteousness" so we may enter heaven without any sin. Just as God gave Adam and

Eve the garments, so He gives us the "garment of faith" today—He does all the work, while we don't do anything to save ourselves. The apostle Paul speaks about this in Ephesians 2:8–9: "For by grace you have been saved through faith. And this is not your own doing; it is the gift of God, not a result of works, so that no one may boast."

> **Man's greatest need— pardon and eternal life— was something only God could give.**

Paul mentioned works in these verses. The Bible is full of laws that tell people how to live. Some laws were for the Israelites in the land of Canaan, relative to their time and space; some are universal for all people, regardless of when or where they live. An example of a law just for the Israelites would be Leviticus 13:45–46, which describes how to deal with a person with an infectious disease so that it will not spread throughout a camp.

> The leprous person who has the disease shall wear torn clothes and let the hair of his head hang loose, and he shall cover his upper lip and cry out, "Unclean, unclean." He shall remain unclean as long as he has the disease. He is unclean. He shall live alone. His dwelling shall be outside the camp.

However, an example of a law that is universal for all people would be Exodus 20:15, "You shall not steal." This is a law for all people, because even in the New Testament, Paul writes to people who aren't Jews, "Let the thief no longer steal, but rather let him labor, doing honest work with his own hands, so that he may have something to share with anyone in need" (Ephesians 4:28).

Laws are necessary in order for people to live together. Even in a perfect setting, God had order. Adam and Eve were told to have children and create civilization. They could eat from any tree but one. God, the ultimate moral authority, had decreed what was acceptable and what was not. There were moral absolutes of right and wrong—Adam and Eve found that out.

> God's Word gives us moral absolutes of right and wrong to know good from evil.

All worldviews have beliefs about how to live, have order, and function under law. Another term for this is ethics, the standards of right and wrong. When it comes to answering questions on how we should behave, if God doesn't exist, there has to be another final authority. If there were no God, we could each decide what is good and bad. This is called moral relativism. The assumption that we're qualified to do this lies in the belief that man is basically good, or neutral at worst, and not sinful as the Bible teaches.

> Moral relativism says morals are relative—each person decides right and wrong.

This sounds really good. We each decide for ourselves what is okay to do. (After all, that was Satan's temptation in Genesis 3:5: "For God knows that when you eat of it your eyes will be opened, and you will be like God, knowing good and evil.") However, the danger of moral relativism is that there is no such thing as wrong, because each person is declaring what he feels is right and wrong. Ultimately, there is no basis for decision making that all can agree on, because it is all based on individual preferences. Or to reiterate what Dr. Provine stated in his debate with Dr. Johnson regarding the philosophical implications of evolution: if evolution is true, then there are no gods, no life after death, no free will, no ultimate meaning in life, and *no ultimate foundation for ethics.* To even debate with someone about good and evil, we must borrow from the Christian worldview!

To show how this concept fails the third worldview test of relevancy, you can demonstrate how no one can actually live as a moral relativist. If people claim we should each decide right and wrong for ourselves, take something from them, like a pen or bottle of water. If they complain, point out the fact you are just employing their worldview of moral relativism and decided you wanted their item. Since there is no ultimate authority, you did nothing wrong.

> **No one can actually live as a moral relativist—believing there is nothing wrong with anything.**

That is why in the past two thousand years there have been three basic theories of human rights used to run governments: Judeo-Christian natural law, social contract theory, and legal positivism.[48] Judeo-Christian natural law says human rights are a gift of God, and any man-made laws that violate those are invalid. We hear this in the Declaration of Independence—"All men are created equal, that they are endowed by their Creator with certain unalienable Rights, that among these are Life, Liberty and the pursuit of Happiness." Here, biblical principles and governmental principles are woven together, so we protect people's rights to own property because "You shall not steal" (Exodus 20:15).

Social contract theory says government is an agreement among individuals to restrict their freedom in order to live together. People get together and decide what they will allow and what they will not. People may decide stealing is wrong and not quote Scripture at all. They simply see it as beneficial to property owners and society at large.

Legal positivism is simply this: the law is whatever the government says it is. If the government wants to take your home and land, it will—the government can even "steal" people, as in the Holocaust. Besides Nazi Germany, this is the basis for other totalitarian states of the twentieth century such as communist Russia and communist China, responsible for over 100 million deaths in the last one hundred years.[49]

So who makes the ethical standards of right and wrong? God? Individuals? The government? Does it matter? Take someone's pen and watch his or her reaction. Or talk to a survivor of the Holocaust, one who could have been exterminated simply for being Jewish. Earlier, we mentioned how evolutionists had difficulty explaining how life came from lifeless matter (scientifically impossible) and how this inanimate matter also had to develop a rational thought process. Remember, it also had to develop a moral code of right and wrong. How is this possible with no ethical foundation? Maybe this explains why Oxford biology professor and staunch atheist Richard Dawkins denies the very existence of good and evil.[50]

If there are simply bad things that happen, how do we determine they were bad in the first place? Is rape bad? According to the University of New Mexico's Randy Thornhill, rape is an evolutionary adaptation in men's genes for reproductive success.[51] Thornhill, a biologist, and Craig T. Palmer wrote a book entitled *A Natural History of Rape: Biological Bases of Sexual Coercion*. Obviously, people reacted against it as a "get-out-of-jail-free card" for rapists since their genes were responsible for their behavior. One Stanford University biologist called it the "evolution made me do it" excuse for criminal behavior.[52]

Yet other evolutionists have said we can choose to fight our evolutionary development from our genetic background, whether it is a predisposition to rape, kill, or steal, if we rebel against these selfish forces. But author Nancy Pearcey points out that "there is nothing in evolutionary psychology to account for this power of choice."[53] Echoing that thought was one of the points in the debate between professors Provine and Johnson on the implications of evolution: if evolution is true, then there are no gods, no life after death, no ultimate meaning in life, no ultimate foundation for ethics, *and no free will, since we are just programmed from our genes to act like rats in a maze.*

So here's the dilemma: a worldview has to tell you how to live as an ethical stance. However, if evolution is true, there is no foundation for ethics, so we each decide right and wrong; yet this doesn't work on a practical level—no society can function this way. The relevancy test has been failed here, which was worldview test number three. And furthermore, if evolution is true, and we evolved from lifeless matter and then gained consciousness, how could we explain evil genes since we have no free will to begin with? This concept fails worldview test number two—it has contradictions.

But if a crime occurs, what should we do? Do we punish the wrongdoer? Does the government seek to protect the victim? There has to be some standard for right and wrong, and someone must establish it—whether it is God, individuals, or the government. This is a universal human need—a need for order and justice. And the Bible explains why we all crave justice in the face of evil—because we all know the basics of God's will. The Law was written on all of our hearts, as recorded in Romans 2:14–15.

> **For when Gentiles, who do not have the law, by nature do what the law requires, they are a law to themselves, even though they do not have the law. They show that the work of the law is written on their hearts, while their conscience also bears witness, and their conflicting thoughts accuse or even excuse them.**

The Christian worldview map matches the reality of our lives—the religion makes sense.

**We crave justice because God's Law is part of us—we know basics of right and wrong.**

People in our world ask, "How can you believe in God with all the evil in the world?" When people ask this question, remember they are using a Christian worldview to even discuss the topic, since there is no basis for ethics in evolutionary thinking. Furthermore, when you deal with real suffering, as in the case of rape, Christians don't point to our genetic makeup and look for a biological excuse. We come alongside the suffering person and offer help, as Jesus did when He walked the earth. Isaiah 53:3–6 prophesied this of the Messiah, Jesus:

> He was despised and rejected by men; a man of sorrows, and acquainted with grief; and as one from whom men hide their faces He was despised, and we esteemed Him not. Surely He has borne our griefs and carried our sorrows; yet we esteemed him stricken, smitten by God, and afflicted. But He was wounded for our transgressions; He was crushed for our iniquities; upon Him was the chastisement that brought us peace, and with His stripes we are healed. All we like sheep have gone astray; we have turned—every one—to his own way; and the Lord has laid on Him the iniquity of us all.

Jesus is familiar with suffering. He suffered as He lived here. He suffered to save us from the greatest suffering of all—eternal separation from God. So how can one believe in God with all the evil in the world? Because the Christian worldview provides a consistent view of reality both in the physical world and the moral one. There is order in the universe and moral order in the world. Planets rotate, and people have a sense of right and wrong. Humans are created beings with the dignity of free will. Who, other than God, and what, other than the Bible, best explain this reality?

Christianity's ethical stance is one of moral absolutes. With our best interests in mind, God told us in the Bible what is permissible and what is not according to His holy and perfect character, giving us the dignity of free will. So the Bible shows us our sin by God's Law—He reveals we have all broken His commands like Adam and Eve did, following the devil's temptation to do things our own way instead of God's way. Yet the Bible also shows us our Savior by the Gospel. This Good News is that through Jesus' perfect life and sacrificial death on our behalf, we can be brought back into a right relationship with God, for which we were created. While we work on earth, using the talents and abilities He has given us to honor Him, the other reason for which we were created, we look forward to seeing God face-to-face in heaven one day. In His presence, "Death shall be no more, neither shall there be mourning, nor crying, nor pain anymore, for the former things have passed away" (Revelation 21:4).

**Our biggest need is met in Jesus, our Savior from sin who reunites us with God.**

So far, we have quoted the Bible many times to prove a point. You may have wondered, "But how do we know the Bible is true?" That's a legitimate question, so let's test this worldview map for accuracy!

# Chapter 6

## Is the Bible True?
### Inspiration of Scripture

According to a 2007 Gallup poll, about one-third of the American adult population believes the Bible is the actual word of God and is to be taken literally—word-for-word.[54] Arguably, the Bible is the world's most important book, since not our only religion, but also philosophy, ethics, education, government, and many other issues derive their answers from it. Therefore, let's turn our attention to this burning question: is the Bible the Word of God?

Christians believe that the Bible is indeed the Word of God and that He inspired writers to compose it. There were approximately forty writers over 1,500 years of time, yet all were writing with one goal—to inform us of our creation, fall, and redemption through the Savior Jesus Christ. So, while there are some forty biblical writers, there is truly only one author—God. When Christians believe in the "inspiration of Scripture," they mean God wrote the Bible, expressing His truth in words of the writers' minds, picked by the Holy Spirit.

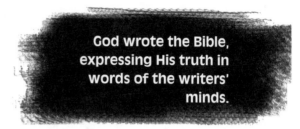

God wrote the Bible, expressing His truth in words of the writers' minds.

In 2 Timothy 3:16–17, Paul says, "All Scripture is breathed out by God and profitable for teaching, for reproof, for correction, and for training in righteousness, that the man of God may be competent, equipped for every good work." Peter adds, "Knowing this first of all, that no prophecy of Scripture comes from someone's own interpretation. For no prophecy was ever produced by the will of man, but men spoke from God as they were carried along by the Holy Spirit" (2 Peter 1:20–21). Yet the writers were not taking dictation since they display different writing styles. (Simply compare Paul's letters to David's psalms!) Nor were they in some kind of trance because they speak of their consciousness in the process as Paul does in 2 Thessalonians 3:17: "I, Paul, write this greeting with my own hand. This is the sign of genuineness in every letter of mine; it is the way I write." In a miraculous way, the Holy Spirit was able to move the writer to use his vocabulary and knowledge in order to communicate God's truth. Dr. Edward Koehler of Concordia University Chicago explained it like this:

> The Holy Ghost not only moved these men when to write but He also suggested, inspired, and controlled what they wrote. The thought content of the Bible, the facts recorded, the truth revealed, the doctrines taught, are in all parts and particulars what God wanted them to write. This is true not only of the things which pertain to our salvation, but also of historical events, of happenings in nature, of personal experiences, and the like.[55]

# Reliability of the Biblical Documents

While God did inspire the original writers on what to write, we do not have any of their original manuscripts in our possession today, most likely because the material on which they wrote did not last. Some of these materials included

- papyrus, which is split reeds laid at right angles and pressed into a paper-like substance;

- animal skins, often called parchment or vellum; and

- wax, clay, or stone tablets.

Copies *had* to be made since the very nature of these materials could lead to their disintegration.[56]

But this leads to another question: if we have no originals, how do we know that what we do have today has been copied accurately? That's another legitimate question!

To test the reliability of the Old and New Testament documents, researchers use what is called a bibliographical test. They are verifying the "writing of the book" by checking what we have today with what the earliest manuscripts say. For instance, some "versions" of the Old Testaments documents researchers examine are the Septuagint (a Greek version), the Samaritan Pentateuch, the Masoretic Texts, and the Dead Sea Scrolls. An examination of the Dead Sea Scrolls, the oldest Hebrew version of the Old Testament we have (which dates back to about 100 BC), reveals astonishing accuracy. For example, the Isaiah scroll is 95 percent identical in a word-for-word comparison.[57] That is amazing! Since the writing material probably would not last, copyists of the text took painstaking steps to insure that what was transmitted was accurate. The Masoretes followed strict regulations to avoid mistakes in copying. These included rules about ink, spacing, and not writing from memory. Once a line was completed, the letters and spaces were counted. If there was so much as a single mistake, the copy was destroyed.[58]

Imagine that—copying something and counting all the letters to make sure you copied it correctly! That's dedication! But when you know it is God's Word, you want to handle it with the utmost respect and care, since it is being passed on to future generations.

What about the New Testament? Some sources say the New Testament has a greater degree of accuracy than any other book from the ancient world, as much as 99 percent.[59] And what is astounding is the *strength* of the argument when comparing it to other ancient writings. When measured against such works as Homer's *The Iliad*, Julius Caesar's *Gallic Wars*, or Plato's writings, there are more copies of the New Testament, written closer in time to the originals, than any other ancient text. To be more specific, contrast the New Testament with *The Iliad*, which records the Greek siege of the city of Troy. There are over 24,000 copies of the New Testament, compared to only 643 of *The Iliad*, the second highest total for any ancient document after the New Testament. As we did with the Old Testament, the New Testament can be verified by checking what we have today with what the earliest manuscripts say.

Next, the time from the earliest known copy of the New Testament after the final book was done is about 225 years, compared to 400 years for *The Iliad*, the second best time gap on the list of writings from antiquity. As more years intervened, more copies were needed—hence the greater possibility for error. Even so, 225 years for the New Testament may sound like a long time, but Frederic Kenyon, librarian at the British Museum, points out that the earliest substantial manuscript copies for the plays of Sophocles were written more than 1,400 years after the poet's death.[60]

We read a play by Sophocles, such as *Oedipus the King*, and don't bat an eye wondering, "Is this *really* what Sophocles wrote?" Nor do we do that for any of the works of Homer, Julius Caesar, or Plato. But we question the Bible. The research shows we shouldn't have concerns for the Word of God as much as for these other works!

Like the Old Testament, we can cross-check the New Testament with various languages in which it was written, such as Greek, Latin, Slavic, Armenian, and the like. If they are all saying the same thing, the text has been accurately transmitted. By verifying what they wrote and what our Bible says, the New Testament passes the bibliographical test. Is the Bible a reliable document? Absolutely—make no mistake about it. Christian apologist Ravi Zacharias points out the large number of supporting documents, the short span of time between the events of the New Testament and the written documents, and the variety of other documents to support or refute Scripture as further evidence of Scripture's accuracy.[61]

> **Cross-checking the oldest sources shows we have the same Bible.**

# Inerrancy of Scripture

So we've established that the Bible is an extremely reliable document, without parallel in ancient literature, passing all bibliographical tests. But some will still say the Bible should be disregarded because it is full of contradictions. To answer these charges, Christians need to know the Bible is without contradiction or error. Another word for this is inerrant. To show this, the Bible must pass an *internal* evidence test. In other words, if you read it from cover to cover, you won't find any contradictions. (Remember worldview test number two.) Besides actually reading the entire Bible, an excellent resource to respond to this charge is the book *Does the Bible Contradict Itself?* by William Arndt.

Christians believe the Bible is inerrant, or without contradiction, because God is the author who inspired the writers. Moreover, there are verses that testify to its perfection, such as Psalm 119:160: "The sum of Your word is truth, and every one of Your righteous rules endures forever." John 17:17 affirms, "Sanctify them in the truth; Your word is truth." Yet people rightfully argue you can't use the Bible to prove the Bible is true. Correct. You must read it from start to finish and look for contradictions. Too often people say, "The Bible is full of contradictions." You should simply respond, "Could you please name one?" Most often you will hear, "Well, I don't know of any off the top of my head, but that's what I've heard."

Here's where you must be ready—remember what Paul told Timothy in 2 Timothy 2:24–26.

> And the Lord's servant must not be quarrelsome
> but kind to everyone, able to teach, patiently
> enduring evil, correcting his opponents with
> gentleness. God may perhaps grant them
> repentance leading to a knowledge of the truth,
> and they may come to their senses and escape
> from the snare of the devil, after being captured by
> him to do his will.

Instead of belittling the person for having no facts to back up the assertion, you could gently instruct him in the hope that God grants repentance leading to a knowledge of the truth—there are no contradictions!

People have been trying to find errors for over two thousand years and have not been successful. The only thing that you *will* find is located in little footnotes at the bottom of the page, which describe variations in manuscripts. These are essentially errors by the copyist. As careful as these men were, they were imperfect people and made slight mistakes, the vast majority of which are spelling or word changes. Remember the Book of Isaiah from the Dead Sea Scroll discussed earlier? It was more than 95 percent the same as the modern Hebrew version of today. The 5 percent variation was mainly slips of the pen and spelling changes. Consider Isaiah 15:9 (NIV): "Dimon's waters are full of blood, but I will bring still more upon Dimon"; the Dead Sea Scroll has "Dibon" instead of Dimon. In fact, the newer ESV translation goes back to the Dead Sea Scrolls to correct the spelling to Dibon. Or consider Isaiah 19:18: "One of these will be called the City of Destruction." The Dead Sea Scroll has "City of the Sun" instead of City of Destruction. That's the extent of the kind of changes you will find if you read the footnotes—your Bible editors haven't hidden anything from you because there is nothing earth-shattering to cover up!

If you read every footnote at the bottom of your Bible that reads, "Some manuscripts say . . ." you will find almost all are spelling or word changes, *but absolutely no doctrine changes or contradictions will be found*. That is incredibly comforting to know, especially when people claim the Bible is full of contradictions. It simply isn't. If it were, people would have found them by now. It's not like unbelievers haven't tried. Dr. Gleason Archer, seminary professor of biblical criticism, writing in the preface to his *Encyclopedia of Bible Difficulties,* said it best:

> As I have dealt with one apparent discrepancy after another and have studied the alleged contradictions between the biblical record and the evidence of linguistics, archaeology, or science, my confidence in the trustworthiness of Scripture has been repeatedly verified and strengthened by the discovery that almost every problem in Scripture that has ever been discovered by man, from ancient times until now, has been dealt with in a completely satisfactory manner by the biblical text itself—or else by objective archaeological information. . . . no properly trained evangelical scholar has anything to fear from the hostile arguments and challenges of humanistic rationalists or detractors of any and every persuasion.[62]

**The Bible passes an internal evidence test— you won't find any contradictions.**

At the start of this chapter we saw that about one-third of Americans believe that the Bible is the Word of God and is to be taken literally. How sad. That is why apologetics and defending the faith is so necessary—people need to know the truth. More people need to know that the Bible is inspired from God, reliably copied, and without contradictions. This map of reality fits the facts and doesn't refute itself, which were basic tests of a worldview. But does God still speak today? Or did He finish with the sixty-six books in the Bible? Let's continue and examine this question next.

# Chapter 7

## What Is the Canon?

Having established the reliability of the Bible by referring to the oldest existing copies to verify what we have in our hands today, let us continue to examine another question: Why are these sixty-six books special? In other words, what is the canon?

The canon is defined as the accepted list of books with authority. Contrary to what you read in *The Da Vinci Code*, the Bible is not a book written by humans, formed by the Emperor Constantine and the Council of Nicaea in AD 325.[63] A committee did not pick the books of the Bible from a vast catalog or library of sources. The books were added through time as a prophet was recognized as God's messenger, and his message from God was written down, collected, and used by people. The Bible starts by God speaking through Moses. He wrote the first five books: Genesis, Exodus, Leviticus, Numbers, and Deuteronomy. As these were saved, they were read according to the command in Deuteronomy 31:10–11.

> And Moses commanded them, "At the end of every seven years, at the set time in the year of release, at the Feast of Booths, when all Israel comes to appear before the Lord your God at the place that He will choose, you shall read this law before all Israel in their hearing."

The Emperor Constantine didn't pick the books of the Bible in AD 325; Moses was writing about 1400 BC, and the Scriptures continued to be added as prophets received messages from God.

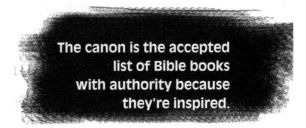

**The canon is the accepted list of Bible books with authority because they're inspired.**

Daniel 9:2 gives us another example of this process of the Bible's growth:

> In the first year of his [Darius's] reign, I, Daniel, perceived in the books the number of years that, according to the word of the LORD to Jeremiah the prophet, must pass before the end of the desolations of Jerusalem, namely, seventy years.

In the Book of Daniel, Daniel tells us he was reading the Book of Jeremiah because it was a message God revealed to Jeremiah. (Specifically, the prophecy was that God's people would be in captivity in Babylon for seventy years and then could return to Jerusalem.) Notice God had spoken a message to Jeremiah; it was written down, collected, and used later by Daniel. Daniel says that this was during Darius's first year in power in Babylon, which was 537 BC. There's no way the Council of Nicaea in AD 325 picked the books of the Bible—the Bible had grown through time! The Church did not create the canon, deciding which books would be called Scripture. Instead, the Church recognized God's inspired Word from its beginning.[64]

When you read the thirty-nine Old Testament books from Genesis to Malachi, that's all God revealed through the prophets. From the fourth century BC onward, the Jews were convinced the prophets ceased to speak, so there was no new word from God.[65] Later, in the first century AD, Philo, a Jewish philosopher, and

Josephus, a Jewish historian, testified about the Hebrew Scriptures we know today as the Old Testament.

> Books were added as God's prophet had a message that was written down and used.

# Jesus and the Old Testament Books

However, some people won't accept that these historical documents support the fact that the Old Testament was already in existence and canonized as the Word of God. Maybe they don't like the content of some of the chapters. Or maybe they don't like the concept of a God out there being the ultimate authority. But it is vital to remember *this fact* when talking to them: Jesus accepted the Old Testament and used it. His books were the same as ours, except for the order and arrangement of some of the books. Most important to recall are these quotes. In John 10:35, Jesus said, "Scripture cannot be broken," and in John 17:17, He said, "Your word is truth." Since the Old Testament is true and unbreakable, Jesus testified to it as God's Word. After His resurrection, Jesus said to His disciples:

> "These are My words that I spoke to you while I was still with you, that everything written about Me in the Law of Moses and the Prophets and the Psalms must be fulfilled." Then He opened their minds to understand the Scriptures, and said to them, "Thus it is written, that the Christ should suffer and on the third day rise from the dead, and that repentance and forgiveness of sins should be proclaimed in His name to all nations, beginning

from Jerusalem. You are witnesses of these things."
Luke 24:44–48

Was the Old Testament accepted by Jesus? You bet! He mentioned "the Law of Moses and the Prophets and the Psalms"—an expression for the three sections of the Hebrew Scriptures, what we call the Old Testament. These Scriptures were from God and prophesied about the Messiah, Jesus. Jesus Himself had no problem with these writings as authoritative, whether composed by Moses or any other prophet, since God had spoken through them.

> **Jesus accepted the Old Testament books as true and unbreakable, the Word of God.**

# The New Testament Books

Since Jesus and the Early Church already had the Old Testament Scriptures, how did the Bible grow to have the New Testament? If you recall, Jesus had twelve apostles whom He taught deliberately and intensively; they were given this charge in Matthew 28:19–20:

> Go therefore and make disciples of all nations, baptizing them in the name of the Father and of the Son and of the Holy Spirit, teaching them to observe all that I have commanded you. And behold, I am with you always, to the end of the age.

Because they were to teach everything Jesus commanded them, any writings by the apostles were saved as important because they were entrusted with passing on the Word of God. This is why the church is pictured as a building: "Built on the foundation of the apostles and prophets, Christ Jesus Himself being the cornerstone" (Ephesians 2:20).

So just as the Old Testament was the inspired Word of God through the *prophets,* so the New Testament was the inspired Word of God through the *apostles.* Yet not all of the writers were actual apostles of Jesus. Norman Geisler notes that apostolic authority, or apostolic approval, was the primary test for canonicity, and not merely apostolic authorship.[66]

> **New Testament books were added as Jesus' apostles wrote messages that were used.**

From approximately AD 100 to 350, there was division over seven books in our New Testament. No one questioned the apostolicity of the four Gospels, the Book of Acts, the thirteen Letters of Paul, 1 Peter, and 1 John. After all, these were written by apostles, or with "apostolic approval." For instance, Mark was a follower of Peter, and Luke researched his Gospel and was an evangelist along with the apostle Paul as he wrote Acts. Justin Martyr, the second-century Christian apologist, records that people would read these New Testament writings in church services interchangeably with the Old Testament, which was a display of their authority from God. "The fact of public reading in the churches became for later generations one of the prime criteria of canonicity ... one might almost say that the church had a canon before she began to think about the canon."[67] Besides Justin Martyr, other second-century Christian fathers referencing the New Testament books include, but are not limited to, Clement of Rome, Ignatius, and Tertullian.[68]

However, seven books were questioned: Hebrews, James, 2 Peter, 2 and 3 John, Jude, and Revelation. For years, the main question was their authorship. The author of Hebrews is not stated, but the message is not contradictory to the rest of the Bible, so it was used.

James and Jude were not apostles but half-brothers of Jesus and later followers, so their works were included later as well. Comparing the writing styles of 1 Peter and 2 Peter reveals two distinct styles, until people settled on the explanation that Peter wrote his first letter with Silvanus's help (1 Peter 5:12), while the second epistle was written by Peter alone. And 2 John and 3 John were short letters, not often cited. They were written by "the Elder," presumably the apostle John due to the language of these letters. Revelation is written by "John," but some questioned whether this refers to the apostle.

Dr. Martin Franzmann said the following in his book *The Word of the Lord Grows*:

> Christianity did not develop from a religion of Spirit into a religion of the Book, as some have claimed. It was from the beginning a "book religion," and the new book, our New Testament, took its place beside the old, not suddenly and magically, but by a gradual process over the years as the church worshiped, did its work, and fought its battles. . . . No commission of theologians, no church council defines the canon or imposes a canon on the church. The canon is not being made; it is growing and being recognized. This remains the case in the fourth century also, when the canon assumed the form it was destined to retain ever after in the Western church.[69]

In the end, around AD 350, the sixty-six books we read from Genesis to Revelation were complete. You may find some Bibles with the Apocrypha included. Norman Geisler points out these books were added by the Roman Catholic Church in 1546 as part of the Counter-Reformation. They were not originally part of the canon due to contrary doctrines, historical anachronisms, and geographical inaccuracies. Interestingly, the Jewish philosopher Philo, the Jewish historian Josephus, and Jesus never quoted them as the Word of God. Also, the New Testament writers and the Early Church did not recognize them as inspired.[70]

At the beginning of the chapter, we mentioned how some people not only believe the Bible is a man-made book, not inspired by God at all, but also that it is a book constructed by a committee of men centuries later in time. Nothing could be further from the truth. We have not only the testimony of the Bible itself, but the witness of historical writings to verify these facts. The claims of Christianity are backed up by the facts. This passes the first worldview test again—it fits the facts. This map is reliable! So from Moses writing Genesis around 1400 BC to John writing Revelation around AD 100, God has spoken through the prophets and the apostles. And since this book is true, then the very first event in the Bible for which we can find evidence of its truthfulness today is the flood. Did God really send a worldwide flood? Did Noah really build a huge boat to survive in it? How did all the animals fit in there? Let's answer these and many more questions in the next chapter.

# Chapter 8

## Was Noah's Flood a True Worldwide Event?

### References outside the Bible

When someone reads the beginning of the Bible, the first events are creation in Genesis 1–2, the fall into sin in chapter 3, the first murder in chapter 4, and the genealogy of the descendants of Adam to Noah in chapter 5. Following these chapters is the flood account in chapters 6–9. The world had become so sinful that God put an end to mankind and started over with Noah and his family. Why was it Judgment Day for all humanity except Noah? Because "The LORD saw that the wickedness of man was great in the earth, and that every intention of the thoughts of his heart was only evil continually" (Genesis 6:5). Yet Genesis 6:9 says, "Noah was a righteous man, blameless in his generation. Noah walked with God."

Emphasizing the reality of this historical event, Jesus spoke about the flood in Matthew 24:38–39 and in Luke 17:26–27, as did the writer of Hebrews 11:7 and Peter in 2 Peter 2:5 and 3:5–6. While there are many references for Noah and the flood *in* the Bible, there are many references to a worldwide deluge in the annals of history *outside* the Bible all over the planet. There are over 270 flood accounts today on major world continents, some with details amazingly similar to the account in Genesis 6–9, which happens to be the longest and most detailed account of all. However, these various versions, with their subtle changes, are best explained as people retold the event, yet lost or changed some of the details as the story was handed down. The following are some examples from around the globe.[71]

The Hawaiians tell of one good man and his family who survived a flood that covered the whole earth that killed all the wicked people. The man's name was Nu-u, and he built a great canoe with a house on it and filled it with animals. The Chinese have a similar account, but more specific. The man's name was Fuhi, and he, along with his wife, three sons and three daughters (not the three sons' wives as the Bible states in Genesis 7:13), survived a flood that covered the highest mountains on the earth. In a Chinese temple's painting depicting Fuhi's flood, a dove with an olive branch in its beak is flying toward the boat, just as the Bible stated in Genesis 8:10–11. The Toltecs of Mexico state that the world lasted 1,716 years before being destroyed by a worldwide flood that covered even the highest mountains. (Their time span of 1,716 years fits the biblical genealogy from Genesis 5.) A few people survived in a "closed chest." Afterward, the people had families and began building a huge tower in case of another flood. However, the language became confused so people wandered from there to other parts of the world. (Goodness, sounds like the tower of Babel from Genesis 11:1–9! By the way, there are nine other accounts like this on the planet similar to the tower of Babel.[72]) The Toltecs claim they started from seven friends and their wives who spoke the same language and traveled together until they settled in southern Mexico, 520 years after the flood.

Why should we bother to know these accounts? Because they verify the Bible as true—the truth fits the facts, corresponding to the evidence we have. Here are over 270 stories from across the planet telling the same account—the event of a worldwide flood, where all perished except the inhabitants of a boat. Coincidence? Hardly! Did all of these cultures just happen to come up with similar stories? Or did the event really happen, and people later told the story, altering parts or omitting details as time went on? What other event do we find repeated hundreds of times with such detail?

> **Over 270 stories from across the planet tell a similar account of a worldwide flood.**

# Questions about Noah's Ark and the Flood

Speaking of detail—the Bible's account of Noah's flood is the most detailed and longest account of all the recorded histories we have. It makes sense since God revealed it to Moses as he wrote Genesis. However, through the years, many objections have been raised against the veracity of the worldwide flood account. An excellent book to respond specifically to those objections is *The Genesis Flood: The Biblical Record and Its Scientific Implications* by John Whitcomb and Henry Morris.

The flood covered the mountains as the other accounts indicate; Genesis 7:19–20 says the water covered the mountains by more than twenty feet. But do we have enough water on the planet to do this? The answer is yes; there is actually enough water in the oceans for covering the earth 1.7 miles deep if all the mountains were leveled and the sea valleys were filled in. In other words, if the planet were as smooth as billiard ball, there's enough water to cover the earth 1.7 miles deep all over.[73] Moreover, the mountains of Noah's time may not have been as high as they are today due to the catastrophic nature of the entire flood and its aftermath.[74] Where is the flood's water today? In the oceans and seas, since three-quarters of our planet's surface is underwater.[75]

> **There's more than enough water on the planet to cover the mountains.**

Meteorologists raise another interesting objection to a worldwide flood. "We don't have enough cloud cover to get rain to fall for 'forty days and forty nights' to flood the earth." That's a valid point, but not what Scripture says. According to Genesis 7:11, "On that day all the fountains of the great deep burst forth, and the windows of the heavens were opened." It wasn't clouds with rainwater that flooded the earth, but possibly a release of massive subterranean waters through seismic and volcanic activity.[76] These waters, under enormous pressure from the earth above it, were released very quickly through some huge earthquake, jetting water into the atmosphere high above. This would also have been when that extra layer of water vapor above our planet (from day 2 of creation) collapsed and helped flood the earth. "Volcanic eruptions associated with the breaking up of the fountains of the great deep could have thrown dust into the water vapor canopy, causing the water vapor to nucleate on the dust particles and make rain."[77]

Another possible explanation is catastrophic plate tectonics. The earth's crust split at lines traversing the globe, possibly due to some enormous earthquake. Besides water bursting forth, the mantle, or the hot rock beneath the crust, rose to fill the voids in the crust, instantly turning to steam cool seawater in the ocean. This in turn formed a line of steam jets that projected significant amounts of seawater into the atmosphere. It fell for forty days as rain.[78] Thus, "The fountains of the great deep burst forth, and the windows of the heavens were opened" (Genesis 7:11). Furthermore, oceans would have flooded continents due to the rising mantle, since the ocean floor itself was rising, as well as the increased water from the "fountains of the great deep." Clouds and their rainwater didn't flood the earth all by themselves—the Bible is clear on this point.

> **The flood wasn't from clouds, but from springs underground and water falling from above.**

Children's books and Noah's ark toys often lead to another objection—how did all the animals fit in there? Genesis 6:15–16 gives us the dimension; the ark was 450 feet long by 75 feet wide by 45 feet high. Imagine a four-story building one and one-half football fields long and you've got the ark! Those dimensions would provide over 1.5 million cubic feet of space, or the equivalent of 520 railroad boxcars.[79] That's a big box in which to store stuff! Noah, his family, and the animals were on the ark for a little over a year (Genesis 7:11; 8:14), so they needed to store sufficient food and water. John Woodmorappe's *Noah's Ark: A Feasibility Study* estimated that less than half of the ark's decks would have been needed for animals and their cages. The rest could be for storage of food, water, and for people.[80] How is this possible? According to Woodmorappe, at most 16,000 animals were needed to preserve the created kinds God had made originally. However, other creation scientists have estimated the number of creatures to be approximately 35,000. In any event, the key is this: "only the parent 'kinds' of these species were required to be on board in order to repopulate the earth. For example, only two dogs were needed to give rise to all the dog species that exist today."[81] Noah did not have to take two of every single species on the planet. Moreover, taking young animals of each kind aboard would be a smart move. They would have required less space, eaten less food, and produced less waste. Furthermore, these juveniles would be able to repopulate the earth after the flood with many more generations than older animals.[82] So the dimensions provide not only ample space for Noah's family, the animals, and supplies, but the dimensions would also provide amazing stability in the water. A ship research study found that the dimensions of the ark were the most seaworthy of twelve ship models tested, combining comfort, stability, and strength. As a matter of fact, the ark's design is so strong that it could handle waves as high as one hundred feet.[83] Another study found the ark's configuration almost impossible to capsize.[84] With 120 years of building experience and the information provided by God to construct the ark (Genesis 6:3, 14–16), Noah did not build a child's toy; it was a huge barge, meant to float for months in an open sea.

**The ark provided ample space for people, animals, provisions, and survival on the sea.**

But even with sufficient space for people, food, and animals, how did Noah and the others care for the animals during the flood? Since they were onboard for a little over a year, wasn't that an overwhelming task? First, we have to remember that the creatures came to Noah according to Genesis 6:20; 7:9, 15. He didn't have to go out and capture them, hauling them aboard. Next, in response to the dark confines of a rocking ship, many animals may have gone into hibernation. Finally, as Woodmorappe indicates, a few farmers can raise thousands of cattle in a small space. With basic devices such as a watering system and food dispensers, it isn't beyond the realm of possibility for eight people to care for thousands of animals for a little over a year on the sea.[85]

**Devices to feed, water, and remove waste may have enabled Noah's family to care for the animals.**

The idea of the ark floating on a planet totally submerged is the biggest objection people have to the flood account. Usually skeptics say Noah's flood was local in scope, limited to only his part of the world. However, if this were true, there would have been no need for the ark to be constructed; Noah and his family could have simply fled on foot to another region. In reality, there was no other escape from humanity's destruction. This is clear from Scripture passages before the flood:

> And God said to Noah, "I have determined to
> make an end of all flesh, for the earth is filled with

> violence through them. Behold, I will destroy them
> with the earth. . . . For behold, I will bring a flood of
> waters upon the earth to destroy all flesh in which
> is the breath of life under heaven. Everything that
> is on the earth shall die." Genesis 6:13, 17

After the flood, Genesis 7:23 states, "He blotted out every living thing that was on the face of the ground, man and animals and creeping things and birds of the heavens. They were blotted out from the earth. Only Noah was left, and those who were with him in the ark." Jesus spoke of mankind's destruction in Matthew 24:38–39:

> For as in those days before the flood they were
> eating and drinking, marrying and giving in
> marriage, until the day when Noah entered the ark,
> and they were unaware until the flood came and
> swept them all away, so will be the coming of the
> Son of Man.

The apostle Peter repeats this concept in both of his letters: "God's patience waited in the days of Noah, while the ark was being prepared, in which a few, that is, eight persons, were brought safely through water" (1 Peter 3:20); 2 Peter 2:5 adds, "He did not spare the ancient world, but preserved Noah, a herald of righteousness, with seven others, when He brought a flood upon the world of the ungodly."

But one of the best arguments against a local flood is the promise God made to Noah. "When I bring clouds over the earth and the bow is seen in the clouds, I will remember My covenant that is between Me and you and every living creature of all flesh. And the waters shall never again become a flood to destroy all flesh" (Genesis 9:14–15). Isaiah 54:9 echoes this thought: "This is like the days of Noah to Me: as I swore that the waters of Noah should no more go over the earth . . ." The God of heaven who flooded the entire earth now makes a covenant with Noah (and all mankind), using the rainbow as a sign of the covenant. He promises never again to flood the whole earth. If Noah's flood were local, this promise makes no sense. God would have already broken His vow countless times, since local floods are a fact of life.[86]

> **The ark's necessity in a worldwide flood is clear from context and repetition; all but eight died.**

If only eight people survived the flood, how did mankind originate from Noah's family? Or some will say it this way: how did we get all the "races"? Actually, there is only one race—the human race. The different groups of people are classified that way by skin color and eye shape, but the basic genetic difference between any two people on the planet is an astounding 0.2 percent![87] We really are basically the same! What accounts for the difference most of the time is the amount of melanin, which gives us our skin color. Knowing this, it is likely that Adam and Eve, as well as the eight on the ark (Noah and his wife; their sons Shem, Ham, and Japheth, and their wives), were middle brown skinned people. A simple exercise in basic genetics show how middle brown parents could have offspring with a variety of skin coloration.[88]

> **If Noah's family was middle brown skinned, their offspring could make a range of colors.**

A final objection raised to the worldwide flood is often stated comically: how did the kangaroos get to Australia? In other words, how did animals migrate over all the continents? This is a legitimate question that can be answered just as legitimately: by the use of land bridges. The remains of these land bridges are still apparent in areas such as the Bering Strait between North America and Asia.[89]

In order to get to Australia, the kangaroos could have used a few options: vast floating mats of logs from trees ripped up from the pre-flood world; people could have taken them there in boats; or the creatures could have migrated on land bridges if sea levels were lower in the post-flood period.[90] The East Indies wouldn't have been a continuous bridge of "stepping-stones" to Australia; it would have simply been a continuous bridge!

Animals migrated mostly via land bridges.

# Geological Implications of the Flood

As stated in the opening of this chapter, the flood is the very first event in the Bible for which we can find evidence today of its truthfulness. While there may be no tangible evidence of Adam and Eve, Cain and Abel, and the rest of the people before Noah, the flood left a permanent mark on our planet even to the present age.

There are four main geologic evidences for the flood. First, fossils of sea creatures are found high above sea level on every continent. Amazingly, even the Himalayas of Nepal, with the highest mountain in the world, Mount Everest, have marine fossils. How can this be? Because Mount Everest, like all other land masses, was under water, as the Genesis account clearly tells us. Earlier, we discussed catastrophic plate tectonics and mentioned the oceans would have flooded the continents. For this to happen, water would have to be added to the ocean, from the "fountains of the great deep" (Genesis 7:11) bursting open due to some enormous earthquake. Furthermore, the ocean floor would have to rise, due to the rising mantle. Consequently, the sea creatures that once lived in the ocean had to be deposited on the continents by a rising sea level.[91] As Psalm 104:5–9 says:

> He set the earth on its foundations, so that it should never be moved. You covered it with the deep as with a garment; the waters stood above the mountains. At Your rebuke they fled; at the sound of Your thunder they took to flight. The mountains rose, the valleys sank down to the place that You appointed for them. You set a boundary that they may not pass, so that they might not again cover the earth.

In this text, the psalmist explains God flooded the entire earth, covering the mountains, until the waters sank into the ocean valleys, running off the mountains. Never again will the waters cover the earth. That's how marine fossils were deposited. The mountains of the pre-flood world were probably not as high as they are today; perhaps only six to seven thousand feet in elevation.[92] Nonetheless, after being deposited there due to the flood, there were significant seismic upheavals that projected the mountains to their present elevations, leaving the marine fossils as evidence of the worldwide catastrophe.

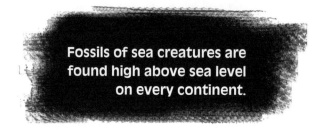

**Fossils of sea creatures are found high above sea level on every continent.**

A second geologic evidence for the flood was the rapid burial of billions of plants and animals all over the planet. This is what you would expect to find in a global catastrophe such as the flood. Quick, how do you make a fossil? Good question. In order to produce a fossil, you need a rapid burial, in the right soil conditions, with extreme pressure. Without these three considerations, organisms will decay and not be preserved.

> For example, soft parts (jellyfish, animal feces, scales and fins of fish) or whole, large, fully-articulated skeletons (e.g., whales or large dinosaurs such as T-Rex) are preserved. Or we find many creatures' bodies contorted. All this evidence shows that these creatures were buried rapidly (in many cases even buried alive) and fossilized before scavengers, micro-decay organisms and erosional processes could erase the evidence. These are found all over the world and all through the various strata.[93]

Notice what is *not* necessary—millions and billions of years. Long periods of time have nothing to do with producing a fossil. When we examine the fossil record, amazing moments are frozen in time, such as one fish eating another, or an ichthyosaur (a marine dinosaur) giving birth! In order to capture these creatures in these situations, they must be buried rapidly in the proper setting with high pressure. The flood would enable these billions of plants and animals to be preserved perfectly.

Furthermore, on viewing these fossil graveyards, researchers often find mixtures of sea- and land-dwelling creatures together, indicating that the flood's torrent swept over both oceans and continents, as we discussed in the previous section. For instance, in Wyoming, one fossil graveyard features alligator, various fish, birds, turtles, mollusks, crustaceans, various insects, and palm leaves. Strange deposits in a state far from the ocean! In Tasmania, clams, snails, and a whale are fossilized alongside a possum.[94]

> **The rapid burial of billions of plants and animals all over is geologic evidence of the flood.**

A third geologic evidence for the flood is that sediment layers, sometimes miles deep, are spread across vast areas and deposited rapidly. One example is the Grand Canyon in Arizona. The rock layers exposed in the canyon walls belong to six very thick, distinctive sequences of sedimentary rock layers that can be traced across the entire continent of North America. In other cases, some sedimentary rock layers can be traced across *different continents.* For instance, the chalk beds of southern England can be traced into other European countries, all the way to the Middle East. Coal deposits stretch from North America to Europe to Asia. These sediment layers were put down rapidly as well; evidence shows that they happened in a matter of hours or days. This fits the biblical record of the flood and the massive geologic upheaval that occurred.[95]

> **Sediment layers that spread across vast areas and deposited rapidly are explained by the flood.**

A fourth geologic evidence for the flood is that rock layers were laid down in quick succession with rapid or no erosion between the layers. In contrast, the dominant view today is that slow and gradual processes required hundreds of millions of years to deposit all the rock layers. If this were true, you'd expect to find examples of weathering and erosion after successive layers were deposited, since millions of years are passing by. However, this is not the case; the geologic record supports the flood account.[96] Again, the Grand Canyon is an excellent example—thick, uniform, horizontal deposits of various sediments resting one upon another from the bottom of the canyon to the top.[97] Folded rock layers in the Grand Canyon and elsewhere show these layers must have been laid down in quick succession and then folded while still soft and pliable, like a stack of thin pancakes over the edge of a plate.[98] The flood's violent upheaval can account for this as well, whereas geologists subscribing to the slow and gradual processes model cannot, since the rock would have been brittle by the time it was millions of years old.[99]

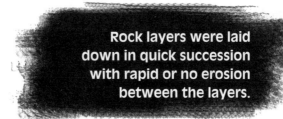

Rock layers were laid down in quick succession with rapid or no erosion between the layers.

# Ark Sightings

Besides geologic evidences of the flood, some believe there is physical evidence of the ark still available to be examined. Genesis 8:4 tells us, "And in the seventh month, on the seventeenth day of the month, the ark came to rest on the mountains of Ararat." There is a Mount Ararat in Turkey, with an elevation of approximately 17,000 feet. This mountain is reportedly one of the most difficult in the world to climb; storms occur nearly every day, with winds up to one hundred miles per hour. The peak is always snow covered; the only months to have some melting of snow and ice near the summit are August and September. These factors seem to be the biggest problem in locating physical evidence of the ark; if it is indeed on Mount Ararat, it would be under snow and ice at a high elevation, possibly 14,000 feet, accessible only a few times a year at best.[100]

Ark sightings have been reported for centuries. Ancient historians who mention the ark include Berosus, a Chaldean historian in 257 BC, and Josephus, a Jewish historian in the first century AD. In more recent times, the Turkish government in 1883 reported that an old ship with stalls and cages was stuck in ice on the mountain. In the early 1900s, George Hagopian claimed the ark was visible after a four-year drought and had broken into two large sections. Czar Nicholas II sent two Russian expeditions to measure and photograph the ark; these results have never been found, presumably lost in the 1917 Revolution that soon followed the expeditions. Three people (among others) claim to have actually seen the ark in recent years: Ed Davis in 1943, Ed Behling in 1973, and Ahmet Ali Arslam in 1989. Due to warm weather and helpful guides, they were able to view the site. They all have been interviewed, with one even given a polygraph (or lie-detector) test to verify the report. Ed Davis passed that polygraph test, yet these individuals do not care whether people believe them or not. They are just sharing their experience because they know the truth.[101]

Besides the high elevation and storms, animals, thieves, and government opposition are major obstacles to climbing expeditions. Recently, terrorists have used the mountain as a staging ground for attacks in Turkey, Syria, and Iraq, so no attempts are scheduled. Aerial photographs and satellite images haven't yielded anything definitive. With numerous eyewitness accounts to something on the mountain, it is hoped that one day researchers will be able to venture up the mountain once again and verify if it is indeed Noah's ark.[102] If an expedition can prove the ark still exists, frozen in snow and ice, it is one more piece of evidence to show the truthfulness of the Bible. But if the ark is never found, it will not change the truthfulness of the account. It would simply mean that the ark has been destroyed after all of these years. What *does* exist are the historical records of a worldwide flood from over 270 other cultures, as well as the geologic evidences of a planetary deluge, providing powerful arguments for the dependability of the Bible as a worldview map.

> **Some claim that Noah's ark is on Mount Ararat in Turkey and can be seen if weather permits.**

But here are some questions that tie into both Noah's ark and the Bible: What about dinosaurs? When did God create them? Were they on the ark? What happened to them? People are curious about dinosaurs. Does the Christian worldview and the Bible even address this issue? Let's find out in the next chapter.

# Chapter 9

## What about Dinosaurs?
### Origin and Size

Dinosaurs are a source of interest as well as confusion. Whether you like *Jurassic Park* or not, you need to know how dinosaurs fit into a biblical worldview. Let's start with some background on the word *dinosaur*. Sir Richard Owen, the most distinguished zoologist in Britain during the mid-nineteenth century, was the first to use the term in 1841. *Dinosaur* means "terrible lizard." You can look in books before 1841, and you won't find the word *dinosaur*; it wasn't yet coined! Until then, "dragon" was the term people used to describe these creatures.[103]

> **Dinosaurs were created on the sixth day, but the term wasn't coined until 1841.**

Where did dinosaurs come from? Since God made all land animals as well as Adam and Eve on the sixth day (Genesis 1:24), these creatures were part of His creation as well. Reading the genealogies of Genesis 5 shows people lived for hundreds of years in the pre-flood world, partly due to a better environment. For instance, Alaska once had abundant tropical plant life, such as mangroves, palm trees, Burmese lacquer trees, and groups of trees that produce nutmeg and Macassar oil.[104] Antarctica was once warm and humid, with great vegetation, as verified by the widespread discoveries of coal and petrified wood.[105] Since reptiles grow as long as they live, it is possible the largest dinosaurs were very old lizards, which lived for hundreds of years as well. However, we tend to think that *all* dinosaurs were gigantic, but this is simply not the case. Based on fossilized remains, the average dinosaur was about the size of a sheep.[106] Dinosaurs could have easily fit on Noah's ark, with the young ones taken for ease in care and for replenishing the earth after the flood.

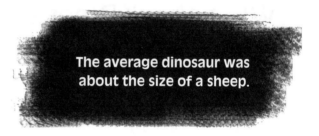

The average dinosaur was about the size of a sheep.

# Extinction?

Following the flood, the world was dramatically changed. The Ice Age brought on a period of glacial activity covering approximately 30 percent of the earth (only about 10 percent is covered with ice today). After the flood, it took approximately 500 years to cover the land with ice and another 200 years to melt the ice back to the existing areas we see today. A likely cause of the Ice Age was the flood itself with its ensuing seismic upheavals and volcanic activity. Volcanic dust and particles would have been in the atmosphere for years following the flood. Ice core samples demonstrate this. With the volcanic debris in the air, sunlight would be reflected back into space, causing cool temperatures over the land masses. Warm water would evaporate and fall as heavy snow over poles, thereby causing the Ice Age.[107] Fossil evidence shows that much of the earth had a tropical climate at one time. Following the flood, major climate changes resulted in an ice age that forever altered the environment and life spans.[108]

The reduction in life span for mankind is apparent based on the genealogy in Genesis 11. But how did this affect the dinosaurs? Since lizards grow as long as they live, a reduction in the life span would also reduce their size. But the biggest change would be in the sheer number of dinosaurs. A changed environment, combined with a lack of food, disease, and man's activity, would cause the dinosaurs whose ancestors survived on the ark to become extinct. These same causes are to blame for creatures being wiped out today, so it should be no great mystery to solve when it comes to the question "What happened to the dinosaurs?"[109] The flood itself destroyed most of these creatures, burying their contorted remains in huge fossil graveyards as a testimony to the deluge about 4,500 years ago.

Bones of a *Tyrannosaurus rex* yielded red blood cells and hemoglobin, even though these should have decomposed long ago if the sample was millions of years old as evolutionists claim. However, this creature wasn't millions of years old—the existence of the red blood cells and hemoglobin testifies to that. Yet the *assumption* that the dinosaur lived millions of years ago was the real problem. As we learned earlier, all worldviews begin with assumptions; moreover, all facts are interpreted by presuppositions as well. One scientist examining a *T. rex* bone noted the presence of blood cells looking remarkably like blood cells found in modern bone.[110] The *fact* of the blood cells in the dinosaur bone is not the issue. How one *interprets* the fact is the key. Isn't it due to the animal being alive recently, only thousands of years ago, and being buried in a massive flood, that accounts for the existence of the blood cells? Doesn't this make more sense than a 65-million-year-old bone with blood cells that should have decomposed?

> A changed environment, starvation, disease, and mankind meant the extinction of some dinosaurs.

# Historical References

Even after losing most dinosaurs in the flood, these awesome animals were not extinct. Some survived from the ark and eventually were the source of dragon legends that we read about today. In the Sumerian story of Gilgamesh, dating to around 2000 BC, the hero killed a dragon found in a forest. As Alexander the Great entered India in approximately 330 BC, he found huge reptiles kept in cages. Chinese culture is well known for dragon stories, while also featuring dragons prominently in their artwork. In England, St. George killed a dragon that lived in a cave in the 1300s. On May 13, 1572, near Bologna, Italy, an Italian peasant named Baptista killed a dragon whose description fits that of a small dinosaur called a *tanystropheus*.[111] Mammoths and flying reptiles like *pterosaurs* have been carved on stone in southwestern areas of America, and the Ica stones of Peru feature *T. rex* and *triceratops*.[112]

Even today there are sightings of large lizards in remote jungles in various parts of the world. Natives as well as explorers have seen mokele-mbembe in the jungles of central Africa.[113]

In December 1999, Papua New Guinea's *The Independent* newspaper reported a "dinosaur-like reptile" seen twice in the Lake Murray area. The creature was described as having a body as "long as a dump truck," nearly two meters wide, with a long neck and slender tail. It walked on two back legs that were as thick as "coconut palm tree trunks" and had two smaller forelegs. The head was shaped like a cow, and it had large eyes and "sharp teeth as long as fingers." The skin was like a crocodile, and it had triangular scoops on its back.[114] So much for the idea that dinosaurs became extinct 65 million years ago! Humans and dinosaurs have lived together since the sixth day of creation. Once again, the evidence fits the biblical worldview map so we can make sense of reality!

**Numerous dragon references are found in history, while dinosaur sightings still occur.**

# Biblical References

Speaking of the Bible, it has references to strange creatures that match the description of dinosaurs. On day 5, "God created the great sea creatures and every living creature that moves, with which the waters swarm, according to their kinds, and every winged bird according to its kind" (Genesis 1:21). The Hebrew word *tannin* means "great creatures"—a great land or sea monster. God may be describing the marine dinosaurs He created.[115] There are many other verses that use the word *tannin*: Psalm 74:13; 91:13; 148:7; Isaiah 27:1; 51:9; and Jeremiah 51:34. But the most interesting biblical references are found in the Book of Job.

In order to show Job His greatness, God asks him to consider two great creatures. The first, *Behemoth,* means "a large beast" as found in Job 40:15–24:

> Behold, Behemoth, which I made as I made you; he eats grass like an ox. Behold, his strength in his loins, and his power in the muscles of his belly. He makes his tail stiff like a cedar; the sinews of his thighs are knit together. His bones are tubes of bronze, his limbs like bars of iron.

> He is the first of the works of God; let him who made him bring near his sword! For the mountains yield food for him where all the wild beasts play. Under the lotus plants he lies, in the shelter of the reeds and in the marsh. For his shade the lotus trees cover him; the willows of the brook surround him. Behold, if the river is turbulent he is not frightened; he is confident though Jordan rushes against his mouth. Can one take him by his eyes, or pierce his nose with a snare?

Hebrew scholars were not sure what the creature was, so they transliterated the Hebrew word *Behemoth* into English. In some Bibles, the footnote will say, "possibly the hippopotamus or elephant," but those animals don't fit the description exactly. Neither has a tail like a cedar tree, nor are they the largest land animals in existence. The very idea of capturing *Behemoth* seems impossible, yet people can snare elephants and hippos. A better explanation of what this creature is would be a dinosaur—possibly a brachiosaur.[116]

Job 41 describes Leviathan, which means "a great water animal." It says, "Can you draw out Leviathan with a fishhook or press down his tongue with a cord? Can you put a rope in his nose or pierce his jaw with a hook?" (vv. 1–2). Later, we read in verses 31–34:

> He makes the deep to boil like a pot; he makes
> the sea like a pot of ointment. Behind him he
> leaves a shining wake; one would think the deep
> to be white-haired. On earth there is not his like,
> a creature without fear. He sees everything that is
> high; he is king over all the sons of pride.

As with *Behemoth,* God was using *Leviathan* to display His glory to Job. And once again, Hebrew scholars transliterated the word, so the footnote reads, "possibly the crocodile." Yet the crocodile doesn't fit the description well enough. People *can* hook them or tie them up. When crocodiles swim in the water, they don't churn up the water like a boiling pot. And you would never say there is no equal to the crocodile on earth—unless this was a huge, crocodile-like creature such as the forty-foot "super croc" *Sarcosuchus imperator* or a large marine dinosaur like a plesiosaur.[117] With both *Behemoth* and *Leviathan,* God showcases the awesome grandeur of His creative power. While elephants, hippos, and crocodiles are good, dinosaurs are even more impressive!

> **The Bible mentions Behemoth, Leviathan, and *tannin*, which were "great creatures."**

We should not be confused by these creatures, nor feel they belong only to an evolutionary worldview. There isn't a gap of 65 million years between dinosaurs and humans as the secular humanist worldview claims. On the contrary, dinosaurs fit perfectly into God's creation along with humans on the sixth day. This is testified to not only in the pages of Scripture, but also in the fossil record, the historical record, and in sightings today. The biblical worldview map makes sense of the reality around us. Moreover, as we proceed, we will see that the Christian message continues to fit the facts when it comes to the most important issue of all—was Jesus of Nazareth a real person, and was He truly the Son of God?

# Chapter 10

## Did Jesus Really Exist?
### General Discoveries in Archaeology

So far throughout this book you have probably noticed there is quite a bit of evidence to back up the claim that the Bible is true; it passes an external evidence test. Renowned archaeologist Nelson Glueck notes no archaeological discovery has ever refuted Scripture; rather, with each new discovery we further confirm the details of Scripture.[118] This statement comes from a Reformed Jewish scholar, not a Christian, and yet he concedes that archaeology supports both Old and New Testament Scripture. In the earlier chapter on worldviews, that was part of test number one—are there facts to support the claim? When it comes to the person of Jesus Christ, the same holds true. There is indeed evidence outside of the Bible for His existence as well as for His divinity. But before we explore these aspects of our worldview map, let's highlight some other noteworthy archaeological discoveries that confirm the Bible's dependability.

We've spent considerable time on the flood evidence and have mentioned the tower of Babel accounts. Another familiar event is Joshua and the battle of Jericho. The destruction of the city and its walls is noted in Joshua 6:20.

> So the people shouted, and the trumpets were
> blown. As soon as the people heard the sound of
> the trumpet, the people shouted a great shout,
> and the wall fell down flat, so that the people went
> up into the city, every man straight before him,
> and they captured the city.

As archaeologist John Garstang dug at Jericho between 1930 and 1936, he found to his amazement that the walls had fallen *outward* so attackers could climb over them and enter the city. Normally, attackers batter walls *inward* after laying siege to a city.[119]

Alexander the Great and King Solomon are among the top two most noted historical figures in antiquity. In other words, if you search for documentation of the most well-known individuals of ancient times, Alexander would be in first place and Solomon would be in second. People from all over the known world were aware of these two great leaders and celebrated their accomplishments in folk literature.[120] Accordingly, 1 Kings 4:34 records, "People of all nations came to hear the wisdom of Solomon, and from all the kings of the earth, who had heard of his wisdom."

After thirty years of study, William Ramsey concluded the books by Luke (his Gospel of the same name and the Book of Acts) are accurate accounts of history. Ramsey calls Luke a first-rank historian, among the world's finest.[121] This makes perfect sense because Luke explains how he did his research before writing his Gospel in Luke 1:3–4. "It seemed good to me also, having followed all things closely for some time past, to write an orderly account for you, most excellent Theophilus, that you may have certainty concerning the things you have been taught." Since Luke had "done his homework," verifying all the information about Christ's life, he wrote this account for a man named Theophilus so he would have complete confidence in believing it as the truth.

The preceding are just a sample of the findings throughout the past two centuries. But now let's turn our attention to Jesus of Nazareth.

Archaeological discoveries show that the biblical record is confirmed and trustworthy.

# Historical References to Jesus

Did Jesus even exist at all? The answer is yes. Evidence for Jesus' life survives in writings outside of the pages of Scripture.

Usually, people associate Jesus with good works and miracles, thinking of Him as being very popular. But the Bible also records that He was a wanted man—in a criminal sense. John 11:57 says, "Now the chief priests and the Pharisees had given orders that if anyone knew where He was, he should let them know, so that they might arrest Him."

Outside of the Bible, evidence for this indictment appears in the Talmud for *Yeshu Hannotzri*, or "Jesus the Nazarene." It says:

> He shall be stoned because he has practiced sorcery and lured Israel into apostasy. Anyone who can say anything in his favor, let him come forward and plead on his behalf. Anyone who knows where he is, let him declare it to the Great Sanhedrin in Jerusalem.[122]

Jesus had a warrant out for His arrest by the Jewish authorities for practicing "sorcery" and "lur[ing] Israel into apostasy," or leading people astray from God. Notice Jesus was accused of sorcery, so His opponents *admitted* He had supernatural ability. However, they simply attributed it to the devil. This fits perfectly with accounts such as Matthew 12:22–24:

> Then a demon-oppressed man who was blind and mute was brought to Him, and He healed him, so that the man spoke and saw. And all the people

> were amazed, and said, "Can this be the Son of
> David?" But when the Pharisees heard it, they said,
> "It is only by Beelzebul, the prince of demons, that
> this man casts out demons."

So we have a *biblical and historical* record of a Jesus who did supernatural things and who was consequently a man wanted by the Jewish authorities.

> **An indictment appears in the Talmud for *Yeshu Hannotzri*, or "Jesus the Nazarene."**

Although not a Christian, Josephus, a first-century Jewish historian, recorded the following:

> At this time there was a wise man called Jesus,
> and his conduct was good, and he was known to
> be virtuous. Many people among the Jews and
> the other nations became his disciples. Pilate
> condemned him to be crucified and to die. But
> those who had become his disciples did not
> abandon his discipleship. *They reported that he had
> appeared to them three days after his crucifixion, and
> that he was alive. Accordingly, he was perhaps the
> Messiah, concerning whom the prophets have reported
> wonders.* And the tribe of the Christians, so named
> after him, has not disappeared to this day.[123]

The italicized sentences in the quote above are believed by most scholars to be later insertions by Christians. However, others, such as Western Michigan University history professor emeritus Dr. Paul Maier, maintain this is the original wording.[124] What is absolutely clear is the fact the historian Josephus, although he himself an unbeliever, records Jesus lived, was wise, good, and popular. This is in accordance with the Bible; take this passage from Luke 6:17–18 as an example:

> And He came down with them and stood on a
> level place, with a great crowd of His disciples and
> a great multitude of people from all Judea and
> Jerusalem and the seacoast of Tyre and Sidon,
> who came to hear Him and to be healed of their
> diseases. And those who were troubled with
> unclean spirits were cured.

After Jesus was put to death by Pilate through crucifixion, His followers continued to be faithful to Him.

> **Josephus says that Jesus
> was wise, popular, and
> killed by Pilate, yet His
> disciples stayed true.**

One such faithful follower was James, Jesus' half brother. Joseph and Mary's sons are listed by name in Matthew 13:55–56. (These are Jesus' half brothers because Mary was His mother, but He was incarnate by the Holy Spirit.) "Is not this the carpenter's son? Is not His mother called Mary? And are not His brothers James and Joseph and Simon and Judas? And are not all His sisters with us? Where then did this man get all these things?" Josephus testifies to the existence of both Jesus and James in this passage:

> Convening the judges of the Sanhedrin, he (the
> high priest Ananus, son of the former high priest
> Annas) brought before them the brother of Jesus
> who was called the Christ, whose name was James,
> and certain others. He accused them of having
> transgressed the law and delivered them up to be
> stoned.[125]

So Josephus, the great Jewish historian, makes two references to Jesus in his writings, although he himself was not a believer. He was simply reporting the facts. Another fact about Christ's life covered in ancient documents is an occurrence during his death. When Jesus was being crucified, the Bible records a darkness covered the land from noon until 3:00 p.m. "It was now about the sixth hour, and there was darkness over the whole land until the ninth hour, while the sun's light failed" (Luke 23:44–45). Thallus, a first-century historian, wrote about this event, but only fragments of his writings exist in the citations of other writers. Julius Africanus, around AD 221, is one who recorded this:

> Thallus, in the third book of his histories, explains away this darkness as an eclipse of the sun— unreasonably as it seems to me (unreasonably, of course, because a solar eclipse could not have taken place at the time of the full moon, and it was at the season of the Paschal full moon that Christ died).[126]

Although the *facts* of the crucifixion and the darkness were not in question, Thallus sought another explanation for the darkness—a natural one, not a supernatural one.[127] Likewise, Julius Africanus also cites Phlegon, another secular authority who dismissed the darkness at the crucifixion as an eclipse. "Phlegon records that, in the time of Tiberius Caesar, at full moon, there was a full eclipse of the sun from the sixth hour to the ninth—manifestly that one of which we speak."[128]

**Both Thallus and Phlegon record the darkness during Jesus' crucifixion.**

Jesus' crucifixion was also documented by the first-century Roman historian Tacitus.

> Christus, the founder of the name (Christians),
> was put to death by Pontius Pilate, procurator of
> Judea in the reign of Tiberius: but the pernicious
> superstition, repressed for a time, broke out
> again, not only through Judea, where the mischief
> originated, but through the city of Rome also.[129]

This is exactly what the Bible records. "So Pilate, wishing to satisfy the crowd, released for them Barabbas, and having scourged Jesus, he delivered Him to be crucified" (Mark 15:15).

> **Tacitus says Pilate had
> Jesus put to death during
> Tiberius's reign; the faith
> spread to Rome.**

While Tacitus called Christianity a "pernicious (or destructive) superstition" and a "mischief," Lucian, who was a Greek satirist of the second century, labeled Christians "misguided creatures" for worshiping the crucified Christ as the Son of God and for living a godly lifestyle.

> The Christians, you know, worship a man to this
> day—the distinguished personage who introduced
> their novel rites and was crucified on that account.
> . . . You see, these misguided creatures start
> with general conviction that they are immortal
> from all time, which explains the contempt of
> death and voluntary self-devotion which is so
> common among them; and then it was impressed
> upon them by their original lawgiver that they
> are all brothers, from the moment that they are
> converted, and deny the gods of Greece, and
> worship the crucified sage, and live after his laws.
> All this they take quite on faith, with the result that
> they despise all worldly goods alike, regarding

them merely as common property.[130]

These "misguided creatures" worshiped Jesus just like the man born blind did in John 9:35–38.

> Jesus heard that they had cast him out, and having found him He said, "Do you believe in the Son of Man?" He answered, "And who is He, sir, that I may believe in Him?" Jesus said to him, "You have seen Him, and it is He who is speaking to you." He said, "Lord, I believe," and he worshiped Him.

After receiving his sight from Jesus, this man saw that Jesus was the Son of God. The later believers saw the same thing and worshiped Him as well.

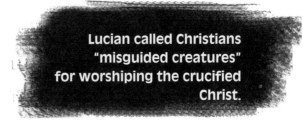

Lucian called Christians "misguided creatures" for worshiping the crucified Christ.

Moreover, these "misguided creatures" were not only persecuted through name-calling, but also through physical means. First-century Roman historian Suetonius mentioned the expulsion of Jews from Rome in *Life of Claudius* 25.4: "As the Jews were making constant disturbances at the instigation of Christus, he expelled them from Rome." Luke recorded the same fact in Acts 18:2: "Because Claudius had commanded all the Jews to leave Rome." After a fire swept through a part of Rome in AD 64, Suetonius noted that "punishment by Nero was inflicted on the Christians, a class of men given to a new and mischievous superstition."[131] What was their punishment? Tacitus gives us the grisly details: "Mockery of every sort was added to their deaths. Covered with the skins of beasts, they were torn by dogs and perished, or were nailed to crosses, or were doomed to the flames. These served to illuminate the night when daylight failed."[132] Besides crucifixion like their Lord, these believers were wrapped in animal skins and fed to dogs or tied to stakes and used as torches for the evening festivities of Emperor Nero.

> **Suetonius said Nero was persecuting Christians; Tacitus records the details of the suffering.**

The persecution of Christians continued elsewhere. In Asia Minor (or modern-day Turkey), Pliny the Younger was writing to Emperor Trajan in the second century, seeking his advice. Since so many Christians had been killed, whether young or old, male or female, Pliny wondered if he should execute only certain ones. Explaining his actions, Pliny wrote that he had found some people falsely accused of being Christian. Upon investigation, they summarily "cursed Christ—none of which those who are really Christians, it is said, can be forced to do."[133] However, the real Christians were simply "guilty" of the following:

> They asserted, however, that the sum and substance of their fault or error had been that they were accustomed to meet on a fixed day before dawn and sing responsively a hymn to Christ as to a god, and to bind themselves by oath, not to some crime, but not to commit fraud, theft, or adultery, not falsify their trust, nor to refuse to return a trust when called upon to do so.[134]

Of what were the Christians guilty? Promising not to lie, steal, or commit adultery, and worshiping Jesus as the Son of God early in the morning through songs. When Jesus Himself was on trial, He admitted He was the Son of God, "But He remained silent and made no answer. Again the high priest asked Him, 'Are You the Christ, the Son of the Blessed?' And Jesus said, 'I am, and you will see the Son of Man seated at the right hand of Power, and coming with the clouds of heaven' " (Mark 14:61–62).

That's why these early Christians could sing to Jesus as the Son of God; He confessed to it under oath! In another case, the apostle Thomas also worshiped Jesus: "Thomas answered Him, 'My Lord and my God!' Jesus said to him, 'Have you believed because you have seen Me? Blessed are those who have not seen and yet have believed' " (John 20:28–29).

> **Pliny says Christians sang songs to Christ as God early in the morning and swore to do good.**

Obviously, not *all* people in the first and second centuries believed Jesus was the Son of God who rose from the dead. But they knew of His life and teaching and made reference to it. A final example comes from Mara Bar-Serapion, a first-century Syrian philosopher who wrote a letter encouraging his son to pursue wisdom. Among other wise, notable figures in history such as Socrates and Pythagoras, Mara Bar-Serapion cites Jesus as an example. "But Socrates did not die for good; he lived on in the teaching of Plato. Pythagoras did not die for good; he lived on in the statue of Hera. Nor did the wise king die for good; he lived on in the teaching which he had given."[135] Jesus' teaching *did* live on in the Great Commission that He gave to His apostles after His resurrection in Matthew 28:18–20:

> And Jesus came and said to them, "All authority
> in heaven and on earth has been given to Me.
> Go therefore and make disciples of all nations,
> baptizing them in the name of the Father and of the
> Son and of the Holy Spirit, teaching them to observe
> all that I have commanded you. And behold, I am
> with you always, to the end of the age."

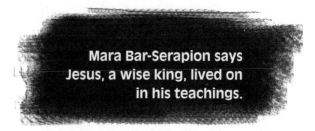

Mara Bar-Serapion says
Jesus, a wise king, lived on
in his teachings.

Miami University history professor Edwin Yamauchi summarizes these non-Christian sources from the first and second centuries, recording Jesus was a teacher from Nazareth and lived a wise and virtuous life. He had enemies who admitted that He did unusual feats they called "sorcery." He was crucified in Palestine under Pontius Pilate during the reign of Tiberius Caesar at Passover time, being considered the Jewish King. He was believed by His disciples to have been resurrected three days later. He had a small band of disciples that multiplied rapidly, spreading as far as Rome. These disciples denied polytheism, lived moral lives, and worshiped Him as God.[136] There are consistent biblical and historical records of the same basic facts about Jesus that are undeniable.

Jesus did exist—
the same basic facts are
found in both biblical and
historical records.

Please remember these facts when people say Christians believe in a fairy tale or myth. Christianity is no myth; there is evidence to support the faith we have. Or you can illustrate your point this way: George Washington is considered to be the first president of the United States. How do you know? By historical documents, accounts, and evidence left behind. Even though no one who is alive today was there to see George Washington, we accept that his presidency was true and real. The same applies to Jesus; our religion coincides with reality, with what really is. There *is* evidence left behind that He did walk the earth, do supernatural things, and die on a cross.

This leads us to the next logical question about Jesus—how do we know He truly rose from the dead? If it is true, the resurrection of Jesus shows us He has conquered humanity's biggest fear—death. All people wonder what will happen when they die; it is one of life's basic questions all worldviews need to address. What is our destiny? Do we die and go to heaven or hell? Do we die and cease to exist? Do we die and come back in another life through reincarnation? Let's continue to seek an answer to these serious questions as we pursue the truth.

# Chapter 11

## What about Jesus' Death, Resurrection, and Their Effects?

### Jesus' Empty Tomb —Unique and Known

In the evidence outside of the Bible for the historical Jesus of Nazareth, there were references to His divinity—that He was considered to be God by His followers. Why would people think Jesus was God? From the previous chapter we saw that Jesus taught large crowds, had many followers, healed various diseases, cast out demons, received worship, and at His trial admitted that He was "Christ, the Son of the Blessed" (Mark 14:61–62). Yet the resurrection of Jesus stands alone as a defining moment to illustrate who He was and is. No other religious figure in history has done this. Abraham, the father of Judaism; Muhammad, the founder of Islam; and Buddha, after whom Buddhists name themselves, did not rise from the dead.[137]

> **Only Jesus rose from the dead; not Abraham, Muhammad, or Buddha.**

Obviously, the Bible records the resurrection. The four Gospel writers state it as factual, as does Luke in Acts 26:22–26, where he records how Paul, on trial for preaching about the resurrection, raised the objective evidence of Jesus' empty tomb in defense of his faith:

> "To this day I have had the help that comes from God, and so I stand here testifying both to small and great, saying nothing but what the prophets and Moses said would come to pass: that the Christ must suffer and that, by being the first to rise from the dead, He would proclaim light both to our people and to the Gentiles."

> And as he was saying these things in his defense, Festus said with a loud voice, "Paul, you are out of your mind; your great learning is driving you out of your mind." But Paul said, "I am not out of my mind, most excellent Festus, but I am speaking true and rational words. For the king knows about these things, and to him I speak boldly. For I am persuaded that none of these things has escaped his notice, for this has not been done in a corner."

Paul states that he is not crazy. What he is says is true—in other words, it is in accordance with reality and the facts. It is also reasonable, and Paul appeals to the king's knowledge of Jesus' resurrection. This was known to the public at large, not just to a select few.

# Anti-Resurrection Theory —The Swoon Theory

Some contend Jesus did not rise from the dead. In fact, some even say that He did not even die on the cross. For example, the Qur'an, the holy book of Islam from the seventh century, says that Jesus did not really die on the cross (Sura IV:157):

> **And because of their saying: We slew the Messiah, Jesus son of Mary, Allah's messenger—they slew him not nor crucified him, but it appeared so unto them; and lo! those who disagree concerning it are in, doubt thereof; they have no knowledge thereof save pursuit of a conjecture; they slew him not for certain.**

However, first- and second-century historical writings we have seen from ancients such as Josephus, Tacitus, and Lucian, all of whom were unbelievers with no religious agenda to forward, state Jesus did indeed die.

Yet skeptics continued to develop explanations on what happened, even though they lived nearly two thousand years later. Karl Venturini, at the beginning of the nineteenth century, suggested the "swoon theory," which says Jesus swooned, or fainted, on the cross, but He did not die. He revived in the cool air of the tomb, escaped from it, and appeared "alive" to people, even though He had actually never died. While notable scholars have debunked this theory, it remains alive in literature and stories today.[138]

**The swoon theory says that Jesus fainted, revived in the tomb, escaped, and appeared alive.**

What have these notable scholars used to debunk this theory? Many arguments can be listed, but consider these facts: after the physical punishment, crucifixion, spearing, and thirty-six hours in a tomb with no medical care, how did Jesus rally enough to open the tomb? How did He then appear to His followers giving the impression He had overcome death?[139]

> **How could Jesus escape the tomb and the guards after the whipping and crucifixion?**

Another question to ask is how could Jesus escape His grave clothes? John 19:38–41 says:

> After these things Joseph of Arimathea, who was a disciple of Jesus, but secretly for fear of the Jews, asked Pilate that he might take away the body of Jesus, and Pilate gave him permission. So he came and took away His body. Nicodemus also, who earlier had come to Jesus by night, came bringing a mixture of myrrh and aloes, about seventy-five pounds in weight. So they took the body of Jesus and bound it in linen cloths with the spices, as is the burial custom of the Jews. Now in the place where He was crucified there was a garden, and in the garden a new tomb in which no one had yet been laid.

Professor Merrill Tenney explains the details of the Jewish burial custom. His body would have been washed, straightened, and then wrapped tightly in bandages a foot wide from armpits to ankles.

> Aromatic spices, often of a gummy consistency, were placed between the wrappings or folds.

> They served partially as a cement to glue the cloth wrappings into a solid covering. . . . How was the corpse extricated from the wrappings since they would not slip over the curves of the body when tightly wound around it?[140]

Remember when Jesus raised His friend Lazarus from the dead, He told people to help Lazarus get out of the grave clothes. "The man who had died came out, his hands and feet bound with linen strips, and his face wrapped with a cloth. Jesus said to them, 'Unbind him, and let him go' " (John 11:44). How could Jesus escape His own grave clothes alone after all the physical punishment He had endured?

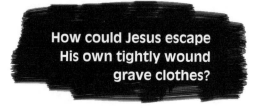

How could Jesus escape His own tightly wound grave clothes?

But the biggest objection to the swoon theory is the fact that Jesus had been pierced in the heart and was indeed dead. The apostle John, an eyewitness to the crucifixion, records this important, yet gruesome detail:

> But when they came to Jesus and saw that He was already dead, they did not break His legs. But one of the soldiers pierced His side with a spear, and at once there came out blood and water. He who saw it has borne witness—his testimony is true, and he knows that he is telling the truth—that you also may believe. John 19:33–35

Alexander Metherell, professor, writer, and consultant for the National Heart, Lung, and Blood Institute of the National Institutes of Health, explains the physical process of crucifixion is essentially a slow death by asphyxiation. The physical positioning on the cross forces the one being crucified to push up with his feet in order to breathe. This went on until the person finally was too exhausted to push up for another breath or until the legs were broken to hasten death.[141]

But what explains the flow of blood and water from Jesus' side when He was pierced with the spear? Dr. Gerard Stanley writes:

> The spear would have entered just below or at the right lower ribs and traveled through the right lung and diaphragm. The tip would have passed through the heart sack, already stretched with pericardial fluid, and entered the right ventricle, which also would have been stretched to capacity from congestive heart failure. . . . As the spear passed though the pericardial sack, thin, watery fluid would have leaked. The passage of the spear tip into the heart muscle itself, as well as into the chamber filled with blood, would have resulted in a gush of blood .[142]

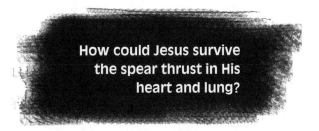

**How could Jesus survive the spear thrust in His heart and lung?**

Piercing through the heart and lung was meant to insure Jesus' death. He didn't swoon or pass out on the cross. If Jesus *had* fainted, the spear thrust would have killed Him instantly. In the 1800s, the swoon theory was a favorite explanation to dismiss the resurrection, but the historical writings by unbelievers recording Jesus' death, archaeological knowledge of Jewish burial customs, and the medical information of crucifixion victims now render it impossible.

# Anti-Resurrection Theory— The Theft Theory

A second theory to explain away the resurrection of Jesus is the theft theory. In this scenario, Jesus' disciples stole His body, hid the corpse, and proclaimed to everyone that He was miraculously alive. This theory is actually as old as the resurrection itself; it is recorded in the Bible in Matthew 28:11–15:

> While they were going, behold, some of the guard went into the city and told the chief priests all that had taken place. And when they had assembled with the elders and taken counsel, they gave a sufficient sum of money to the soldiers and said, "Tell people, 'His disciples came by night and stole Him away while we were asleep.' And if this comes to the governor's ears, we will satisfy him and keep you out of trouble." So they took the money and did as they were directed. And this story has been spread among the Jews to this day.

The trouble with this theory is the guards were there to prevent the disciples from doing this in the first place. See Matthew 27:62–66:

> The next day, that is, after the day of Preparation, the chief priests and the Pharisees gathered before Pilate and said, "Sir, we remember how that impostor said, while He was still alive, 'After three days I will rise.' Therefore order the tomb to be made secure until the third day, lest His disciples go and steal Him away and tell the people, 'He has risen from the dead,' and the last fraud will be worse than the first." Pilate said to them, "You have a guard of soldiers. Go, make it as secure as you can." So they went and made the tomb secure by sealing the stone and setting a guard.

Since the guards had been charged with one duty—prevent Jesus' disciples from stealing His corpse—to fail in that solitary assignment was inexcusable. Stranger still is the logic of their excuse for not doing their job: "His disciples came by night and stole Him away while we were asleep" (Matthew 28:13). If the soldiers had been sleeping, how could they know who stole the body?[143]

> **If the soldiers were sleeping, how could they know who stole the body?**

Furthermore, to actually fall asleep while on watch meant the death penalty for Roman soldiers.[144] That's why the chief priests and elders devised a plan and gave the soldiers a bribe to say that they were asleep. "And if this comes to the governor's ears, we will satisfy him and keep you out of trouble" (Matthew 28:14). If the guards had actually been negligent in their duty, they should have been executed; instead, they took hush money to say they slept while the disciples snuck past them and took the corpse that they were guarding, which was their sole mission.

> **If the guards had actually been sleeping on duty, they should have been executed.**

What also makes the theft theory unbelievable is the actions of the disciples. When Jesus was arrested in the Garden of Gethsemane, Mark 14:50 says the disciples "all left Him and fled" because of the "crowd with swords and clubs, from the chief priests and the scribes and the elders" (Mark 14:43). At Jesus' trial, only Peter and John were nearby (John 18:15–16). During the crucifixion, all the apostles except John had hidden for fear of arrest and possible punishment. Contrast these actions with the theft theory: bold and daring disciples face enormous odds to steal their beloved Master's body from a heavily guarded tomb. Yet imagine for a moment the disciples *did* sneak past sleeping guards, roll away the stone without awakening anyone, and abscond with Jesus' remains. The disciples would go on to preach lies about the resurrection of Jesus, and later, each of the apostles, with the exception of John, would die a martyr's death. Peter was crucified upside down. Bartholomew was skinned alive and crucified. If the resurrection were not true, this suffering does not make any sense. Why would the disciples choose to die for a lie?

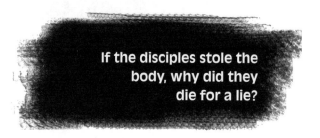

If the disciples stole the body, why did they die for a lie?

In the end, the empty tomb of Jesus has only two explanations: it was either the work of humans or of God. If Jesus' body was removed by humans, His enemies could not have done it; they would have had no motive to remove His body and say that He was alive. Jesus' friends could not have done it for reasons listed above—why die for a lie? The most logical explanation is that Jesus' empty tomb was the work of God.[145]

# Anti-Resurrection Theory —The Hallucination Theory

A third theory to address Christ's resurrection is the hallucination theory. It proposes the disciples *thought* they saw Jesus alive; in other words, it was all just an illusion or a figment of their imagination.

There are a number of problems with this theory. Normally,

hallucinations are rare and are caused by drugs or bodily deprivation. Furthermore, they require a mind full of expectation or anticipation, not fear and anxiety. The apostles would not be good candidates for hallucinations.[146]

> **Full of fear and anxiety, the apostles would not be good candidates for hallucinations.**

The problem is hallucinations are individual events; they happen to only one person at a time. There's no such thing as a group hallucination, nor can one person induce his hallucination in others.[147]

These psychological principles are major obstacles to this theory, since there are many accounts of Jesus appearing to numerous people who report seeing the same thing. Besides Jesus' appearances to the disciples in the Gospels, take this record from 1 Corinthians 15:3–8:

> For I delivered to you as of first importance what I also received: that Christ died for our sins in accordance with the Scriptures, that He was buried, that He was raised on the third day in accordance with the Scriptures, and that He appeared to Cephas, then to the twelve. Then He appeared to more than five hundred brothers at one time, most of whom are still alive, though some have fallen asleep. Then He appeared to James, then to all the apostles. Last of all, as to one untimely born, He appeared also to me.

Paul not only lists individuals who saw Jesus alive such as himself, James, and Peter, but he also states that "the twelve," "all the apostles," and "more than five hundred brothers at one time" saw

Him. Experts note that hallucinations aren't something seen by a group of people.

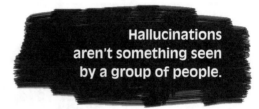

Hallucinations aren't something seen by a group of people.

Besides the fact many people saw Jesus alive after the resurrection, there was physical interaction with Him. Thomas touched Jesus' nail-pierced hands and spear-torn side in John 20:24–28.

> Now Thomas, one of the Twelve, called the Twin, was not with them when Jesus came. So the other disciples told him, "We have seen the Lord." But he said to them, "Unless I see in His hands the mark of the nails, and place my finger into the mark of the nails, and place my hand into His side, I will never believe."

> Eight days later, His disciples were inside again, and Thomas was with them. Although the doors were locked, Jesus came and stood among them and said, "Peace be with you." Then He said to Thomas, "Put your finger here, and see My hands; and put out your hand, and place it in My side. Do not disbelieve, but believe." Thomas answered Him, "My Lord and my God!"

In Luke 24:36–43, Jesus proves His corporeal reality by eating in front of the apostles:

> As they were talking about these things, Jesus Himself stood among them, and said to them,

> "Peace to you!" But they were startled and
> frightened and thought they saw a spirit. And He
> said to them, "Why are you troubled, and why do
> doubts arise in your hearts? See My hands and
> My feet, that it is I myself. Touch Me, and see. For
> a spirit does not have flesh and bones as you see
> that I have." And when He had said this, He showed
> them His hands and His feet. And while they still
> disbelieved for joy and were marveling, He said to
> them, "Have you anything here to eat?" They gave
> Him a piece of broiled fish, and He took it and ate
> before them.

But some of the strongest evidence for the resurrection comes from the testimony of the women who went to the tomb on that Sunday morning.

> So they departed quickly from the tomb with fear
> and great joy, and ran to tell His disciples. And
> behold, Jesus met them and said, "Greetings!"
> And they came up and took hold of His feet and
> worshiped Him. Then Jesus said to them, "Do not
> be afraid; go and tell My brothers to go to Galilee,
> and there they will see Me." Matthew 28:8–10

**People interacted with Jesus in many ways; some were touching Him and eating food with Him.**

This is powerful for two reasons. First, groups of women physically touched the feet of the risen Christ, thereby showing this was no hallucination. Second, the first eyewitnesses of the resurrected Jesus were females, not males. In first-century Jewish society, women were held in low regard. Professor and author William Lane Craig says that rabbinical writings testify to the low esteem of women with entries such as, "Let the words of the Law be burned rather than be delivered to women," and "Blessed is he whose children are male, but woe to him whose children are female." Since females had such poor standing in society, a woman's testimony was regarded as worthless—they were not even allowed to serve as witnesses in a Jewish court. Dr. Lane notes that the Gospel writers reported women as the first witnesses of the resurrection. This certainly went against the cultural standard. Yet they faithfully recorded what happened despite the potentially embarrassing cultural reaction.[148]

Jesus appeared to the apostles as well. Peter testified to this again and again in the Book of Acts. In Acts 2:32, Peter preached to a crowd saying, "This Jesus God raised up, and of that we all are witnesses." Peter reiterated this in Acts 3:15. Speaking to another group, he said, "You killed the Author of life, whom God raised from the dead. To this we are witnesses." Addressing a man named Cornelius in Acts 10:41, Peter said, "Not to all the people but to us who had been chosen by God as witnesses, who ate and drank with Him after He rose from the dead." If these were all hallucinated experiences, the Jewish religious leaders of the day could have stopped Christianity in its infancy. In order to put an end to this resurrection preaching, Jesus' opponents would simply have had to go to the tomb and shown everyone the body. This would have proved the disciples were merely hallucinating or lying and were not to be trusted.

> If the disciples were hallucinating, the opponents would simply have had to go to the tomb.

# Conquering Humanity's Biggest Fear

But the disciples *can* be trusted. We've already seen the Bible is a reliable document, accurately copied and transmitted through the centuries. Armed with this information, what can we know about that first Good Friday and Easter Sunday? Jesus did die; there is sufficient evidence for that both inside and outside of the Bible. Jesus' tomb was indeed empty; His enemies wouldn't have stolen the body, nor would have the disciples. Jesus' disciples and others saw Him and interacted with Him after the resurrection; all of the apostles except John would die a martyr's death for this knowledge.

> **Jesus' resurrection was a real event in history, not a mythical idea.**

Since Jesus' resurrection was a real event in history, not a mythical idea, does this affect the rest of us? The answer is yes. As stated earlier, all worldviews need to answer fundamental questions of origin, purpose, and destiny. In other words, where did we come from, why are we here, and what happens when we die? Christianity has answers to all of those questions with solutions that fit reality and the world around us. We live in a divinely designed world of both physical and moral order that has decay and death in it; the creation and the fall into sin account for this fact. We live with a desire to find meaning in our lives, and yet even our accomplishments fail to fill a void that only God can fill; Jesus Christ satisfies our longing by bringing us back into a harmonious relationship with God, because by faith in Him our sin is removed. We live with death all around us; because of Adam's sin, death entered the world. It was because of mankind's sin that Jesus Himself entered the world. Born in a lowly stable, the God of this universe took on human flesh and lived perfectly among us, fulfilling the righteousness His Law requires. Then Jesus willingly went to the cross, paying the punishment for our sins so we may be set free. Jesus was raised from the dead. We will be raised too. There is hope in the midst of suffering and death. Jesus has conquered our biggest fear—death.

> **Jesus' resurrection is proof He has conquered our biggest fear—death.**

Listen to Jesus Himself deal with this issue of our destiny—what will happen when we die. Speaking to Martha at the grave of her brother Lazarus, Jesus said:

> "I am the resurrection and the life. Whoever believes in Me, though he die, yet shall he live, and everyone who lives and believes in Me shall never die. Do you believe this?" She said to Him, "Yes, Lord; I believe that You are the Christ, the Son of God, who is coming into the world." John 11:25–27

Jesus said this to comfort Martha (and her sister Mary) after their brother died, acknowledging Lazarus would rise on Judgment Day. Yet Jesus went one step further. He didn't wait until Judgment Day; Jesus raised Lazarus from the dead that very day, proving He was the Christ, the Son of God, the resurrection and the life.

Interestingly, Lazarus has two tombs on the planet. One is in Bethany, not far from Jerusalem in Israel. That town is now called Azariyeh or Lazariyeh, meaning "the place of Lazarus," to mark this significant event.[149] The other tomb is on the island of Cyprus in the Mediterranean Sea. It says, "Lazarus, bishop of Larnaca. Four days dead. Friend of Jesus."[150] This inscription fits the account in John that he was Jesus' friend (John 11:1–3) and was dead for four days (v. 39). But even more amazing is the fact Lazarus lived again after his first death! His second tomb is a testimony to this fact. Lazarus is a reminder to all of us that Jesus has conquered death, because He is the resurrection and the life.

Notice Jesus called Himself the resurrection, not the reincarnation. We are not reincarnated, with our souls returning to live in other bodies. Ecclesiastes 12:7 says the body "returns to the earth as it was, and the spirit returns to God who gave it." Furthermore, Hebrews 9:27–28 says, "And just as it is appointed for man to die once, and after that comes judgment, so Christ, having been offered once to bear the sins of many, will appear a second time, not to deal with sin but to save those who are eagerly waiting for Him." The Bible says we die *once* and then face God's judgment.

> Jesus is the resurrection;
> The Bible says we die once
> and face judgment, not
> reincarnation.

On Judgment Day, facing an eternity either with God or without Him depends on our faith, or lack thereof, in Christ. Jesus said:

> For God so loved the world, that He gave His only Son, that whoever believes in Him should not perish but have eternal life. For God did not send His Son into the world to condemn the world, but in order that the world might be saved through Him. Whoever believes in Him is not condemned, but whoever does not believe is condemned already, because he has not believed in the name of the only Son of God. John 3:16–18

The apostle John wrote the same thing in 1 John 5:11–13.

> And this is the testimony, that God gave us eternal life, and this life is in His Son. Whoever has the Son

has life; whoever does not have the Son of God does not have life. I write these things to you who believe in the name of the Son of God that you may know that you have eternal life.

> **On Judgment Day, facing eternity either with or without God depends on our faith in Christ.**

Since we don't just die and cease to exist, answering the question "Who was Jesus?" has eternal consequences. The great Christian apologist, professor, and author C. S. Lewis developed the "Lord, liar, or lunatic" trilemma to get people to think through this issue of Jesus' identity.

I am trying here to prevent anyone saying the really foolish thing that people often say about Him: "I'm ready to accept Jesus as a great moral teacher, but I don't accept His claim to be God." That is the one thing we must not say. A man who was merely a man and said the sort of things Jesus said would not be a great moral teacher. He would either be a lunatic—on a level with the man who says he is a poached egg—or else he would be the Devil of Hell. You must make your choice. Either this man was, and is, the Son of God: or else a madman or something worse. You can shut Him up for a fool, you can spit at Him and kill Him as a demon; or you can fall at His feet and call Him Lord and God. But let us not come with any patronizing nonsense about His being a great human teacher. He has not left that open to us. He did not intend to.[151]

What C. S. Lewis was basically saying was this: Logically, we know Jesus was no legend. He really lived. So He was either the Lord, as He claimed to be at His trial and elsewhere, or He was a liar, claiming that He could give eternal life to people (like Mary and Martha), or He was a lunatic, thinking He was God. The problem with saying that Jesus wasn't the Lord leaves you with Him as either a liar or a lunatic. If He was a liar, then don't list Him as a great moral teacher or role model for all of us, since He deceived people with blatant lies and false hope. If He was a lunatic, why do none of His teachings and actions fit such a diagnosis? Even unbelieving historians agree that He was a positive force in the community. Remember Josephus said, "At this time there was a wise man called Jesus, and his conduct was good, and he was known to be virtuous."[152] If He wasn't a liar or a lunatic, Jesus must be the Lord, as the apostle Peter understood when asked by Jesus in Matthew 16:15–17.

> He said to them, "But who do you say that I am?" Simon Peter replied, "You are the Christ, the Son of the living God." And Jesus answered him, "Blessed are you, Simon Bar-Jonah! For flesh and blood has not revealed this to you, but My Father who is in heaven."

Later, when Jesus asked the apostles if they were going to leave Him, Peter went on to confess, "Lord, to whom shall we go? You have the words of eternal life, and we have believed, and have come to know, that You are the Holy One of God" (John 6:68–69).

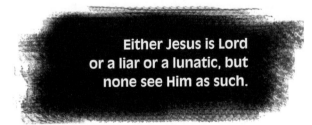

Either Jesus is Lord or a liar or a lunatic, but none see Him as such.

# "Do" Religions versus a "Done" Religion

Peter knew it was futile to leave Jesus; He was the Savior and had the way of eternal life. While other religions exist on earth, none is more popular than Christianity. About one-third of all people are Christians.[153] Yet something else is distinctive about the faith. In all other religions, you "do" something for salvation. You must be good, keep enough laws, or satisfy certain requirements. The pressure of salvation is on you. Contrast that with Christianity. One unique aspects of Christianity is salvation. It is "done" for you by Christ; there is nothing you can do to merit entry into heaven. No other religion on the planet shares this concept. This is made perfectly clear in Ephesians 2:8–9: "For by grace you have been saved through faith. And this is not your own doing; it is the gift of God, not a result of works, so that no one may boast." That's why the apostle John, near the end of his gospel, wrote these lines:

> Now Jesus did many other signs in the presence
> of the disciples, which are not written in this book;
> but these are written so that you may believe
> that Jesus is the Christ, the Son of God, and that
> by believing you may have life in His name. John
> 20:30–31

Simply by believing Jesus is the Christ, the Son of God, you may have life in His name, just as Lazarus did. Lazarus didn't do anything; he couldn't since he was dead. Jesus had to raise him from the dead. In the same way, we are spiritually dead in sin, and God raises us up by the Holy Spirit's power. That's why Ephesians 2:4–5 says, "But God, being rich in mercy, because of the great love with which He loved us, even when we were dead in our trespasses, made us alive together with Christ—by grace you have been saved." We don't do anything; how could we, since we're spiritually dead? Salvation is done for us.

> **In all other religions you do something for salvation; through Christ, it is done for you.**

What a comfort to know this worldview not only matches the reality around us, fitting the facts, but it also answers the questions all people have and is useful in dealing with the issues of suffering and death. The Lord of Life dealt with our biggest fear and overcame it. Christ is risen! He is risen indeed! It is true! Yet more and more today, people don't believe that the issue of absolute truth is even possible. Everyone can have his own worldview map that is true for him; there is no absolute truth for all people. Is this true— there is no truth? Let's examine this topic in our next chapter.

# Chapter 12

## What Is Postmodernism and the New Tolerance?

### Historical Perspective

Earlier in the book, I mentioned you are free to believe what you want, but the real question would be, is it true? According to the dictionary, truth is defined as "Conformity to knowledge, fact, actuality, or logic."[154] You could *believe* something, accepting it as true, genuine, or real, but that wouldn't make it *true*. Take, for example, the idea that there's a man in the moon. You are free to believe this statement, but it doesn't fit the facts and correspond to reality—just check out NASA's findings from their moon missions.

Now compare the belief about a man in the moon with the belief in the resurrection of Jesus. The resurrection does match reality and conform to logic and facts. By everything we've seen in the last chapter, the resurrection is true!

Yet today, the very issue of truth itself is under fire. Some say there is no truth. Others say what is true for them may not be true for you. What does this mean? In order to give a name to this demotion of truth, scholars say we are living in postmodern times. But what does *this* mean? And for that matter, what would pre-modern, or modern, times be? Let's gain some perspective on these three eras, pre-modern, modern, and postmodern times, by traveling through history to see how people have generally viewed three key issues: the supernatural, the account of how we came to be in existence, and the issue of truth.[155]

In what could be called the pre-modern era, or before the 1600s, there was a strong belief in the supernatural, namely, God. Furthermore, people viewed oral and written traditions, such as the Bible, as having authority to explain all of reality. The Bible gave us the explanation of where we came from, why we're here, and what happens in the end. It is a "big story," or meta-narrative, an overarching explanation of what constitutes reality.[156] For the pre-modern person, truth is objective, corresponding to reality, and may be known through the Bible or through reason. Truth is what you observe in the real world and statements made about that world.[157] The statement "The moon orbits the earth" is an example of a truth statement corresponding to reality.

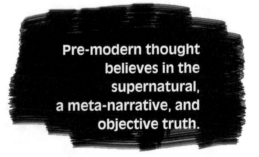

**Pre-modern thought believes in the supernatural, a meta-narrative, and objective truth.**

Entering the modern period from approximately 1600 to 1960, skepticism concerning the supernatural grew. This is not to say all people abandoned their belief in God altogether; for some there was doubt, while for others there was total disbelief and a falling away from the faith. What replaced God was reason and science. Science would give humanity the big story of all reality—the explanation of where we came from, why we're here, and what happens in the end. Evolution, the big bang, and the accompanying theories stem from this time. What remains consistent from the pre-modern time, however, is an attitude toward the truth; it is still objective, corresponding to reality, and may be known by discovering facts about the world.

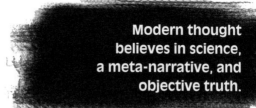

Modern thought
believes in science,
a meta-narrative, and
objective truth.

However, today's postmodern period, stemming from 1960 on, seems to have problems with any claims to knowledge and truth. Not only is the supernatural dismissed, but science is as well. There is a rejection not only of creation but also of evolution to give us the big story of all reality. There is no meta-narrative, an overarching story that defines reality. No one was there to see either the first day of creation or the big bang, so nobody knows. We can't know. Truth and reality are subjective, not objective. You create them. In addition, truth and reality are also constructed by societies, and all societies are different, so there are different truths. Postmodernism's most famous expression is "That's true for you, but not for me." It was the first cultural change based on a shift in the source of truth, not some scientific discovery or medical breakthrough.

Postmodern thought
says there is no God,
no meta-narrative,
and no objective truth.

This postmodern worldview permeates everything—schools, movies, television, music, government—often without our awareness. Let's try to summarize the claims of postmodernism so they are more readily discerned, and we will note problems with this philosophy.

# Postmodern Claims and Contradictions

A summary of postmodern claims would include the following. There is no truth, just interpretations by different people and cultures, and all are equally valid. Take the resurrection of Jesus as an example. In postmodern thought, the "Christian truth" is Jesus rose from the dead, while in the "Muslim truth," He didn't even die on the cross, let alone rise from the dead. David Noebel states it this way: "There is no universal Truth (capital *T*); there are only "truths" (small *t*) that are particular to a society or group of people and limited to individual perception."[158] These small *t* truths would encompass religion, science, education, and anything else related to particular cultures, which are arbitrary beliefs societies have conditioned their people to accept.[159]

> There is no truth, just interpretations by different people and cultures, and all are equally valid.

But did you notice a contradiction in this worldview? Remember our second test for a worldview is that it doesn't have contradictions. If something is logically inconsistent, it cannot be true. In the example of the resurrection, there is an obvious contradiction—the Christian and Muslim both cannot be right. Did Jesus die or didn't He? Did He rise from the dead or didn't He? As for the postmodern claim there are no universal truths, just cultural ones, even secular humanists disagree, for they claim science as a universal truth no matter their background.[160] For example, no matter where you go, people die, two plus two equals four, and the moon goes through phases.

Greater still is the larger contradiction within the postmodern worldview claim that there is no truth. Proposing there is no truth *is* a truth statement. Thus the postmodernist reveals a self-defeating position because its own claim must be included in the statement "There is no truth." It is inconsistent to say, "The truth is, there is no truth." Or to put it a different way, Nancy Pearcey wrote:

The key slogan of postmodernism is "Truth is made, not found." . . . Beliefs are merely human constructions, like the gadgets of modern technology. . . . The most devastating argument we can use against this radical reductionism is that it undercuts itself. If ideas and beliefs are not true but only useful for controlling the environment, then that applies to the idea of postmodernism itself. And if postmodernism is not true, then why should the rest of us give it any credence?[161]

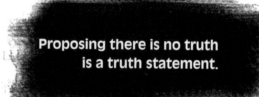

**Proposing there is no truth is a truth statement.**

A second claim of postmodernism is that there are no meta-narratives, or big stories, to explain all reality, whether the model is creation or evolution. Creation is discarded since God doesn't exist, the assumption with which postmodernism begins. (Remember all worldviews begin with an assumption: either God exists or He doesn't.) In addition, the big bang theory is dismissed because scientists weren't there to see the origin of the universe, so "statements reflecting the whole world are impossible . . . only *local* stories told by various cultures" explain the world.[162]

Yet here's another contradiction in postmodernism. Proposing there are no meta-narratives is another truth statement, which is inconsistent in a system that says there is no truth. If there's no truth, how can we be told authoritatively that only local stories told by various cultures are permissible? Who is to say there is no big story?

A third claim in postmodernism would be any written text has no real meaning, just various interpretations open to readers. The phrase most commonly heard associated with this mind-set would be "What does this mean to you?" In postmodernism, each writer has his own cultural setting, but the reader's interpretation of the text is more important than the actual writing.[163] Professor

J. P. Moreland explains it this way:

> Rather, the meaning of a text, according to postmodernists, is determined by a community of readers who share an interpretation. Thus Paul's intentions are irrelevant to the meaning of the book of Romans. In fact, there *is* no book of Romans. Rather, there's a *Lutheran* book of Romans, a *Catholic* book of Romans, a *Marxist* book of Romans, and so on — but no book of Romans in itself.[164]

However, this flies in the face of the Lutheran interpretation of Scripture: "A Scripture text can have but one divinely intended sense and meaning; two contradictory interpretations of the same text cannot both be correct."[165] Take John 14:6 as an example: "Jesus said to him, 'I am the way, and the truth, and the life. No one comes to the Father except through Me.'" How many interpretations are there for this clear statement?

Here's the contradiction: when we're asked to agree with postmodernism's interpretation that there is nothing but interpretations of written texts, it's not open to debate—that is truth! But in a worldview that says there is no truth, how is this possible? Furthermore, Professor D. A. Carson said he never met a postmodern author who was happy when a reviewer misinterpreted his work.[166] These authors don't practice what they preach. There *is* a real meaning behind a text. You cannot just interpret how you want.

> We're asked to agree with the interpretation that there's nothing but interpretations.

And while the freedom to interpret words as we want has

appeal, especially when it comes to ones for which we don't care, reality has a tendency to slap us in the face. If someone says, "The hall is on fire," there *may be* various interpretations to the sentence. But the statement that fits a real world of smoke and flames in the hallway is not open to multiple interpretations. A burning hall is not a matter of word games. With the correspondence theory of truth, the truth corresponds to the facts of reality, and people can get hurt.

# Postmodernism's Antirealism

And that's the biggest problem with postmodern thought today—it runs smack dab into reality. Not only do postmodern proponents claim you can create your own meaning to written words, but they also state that you construct your own world according to your culture and experience. According to the postmodernist, all of us are conditioned by our society and language, and no one is actually free to engage a universe with objectively true statements of fact. All thinking is a "social construct," or arbitrary beliefs that we have been conditioned to accept by our culture, just as others have been conditioned by their culture.

Using the resurrection example again, the Christians have been conditioned to believe their truth, just as the Muslims have been conditioned to believe their truth. It doesn't matter what objective sources such as first- and second-century writings from Josephus, Tacitus, and Lucian say about Jesus' death; if the Muslim says Jesus did not die, then that is true for them. The Christians have their truth, and the Muslims have their own. The correspondence theory of truth, that statements correspond to the objective, real world, has no place in the domain of postmodern thought, where reality is subjectively constructed by human thought. This is called antirealism.

> **Antirealism is where reality is subjectively constructed by human thought.**

Another example of this would be abortions and fetal homicides. When a woman is pregnant, she is able to abort the fetus, and no crime is committed. However, if an attacker kills a pregnant woman, the accused could be charged also with fetal homicide—that is, with two murders. and not just the mother's. At least thirty-five states recognize the unlawful killing of an unborn child as homicide in at least some circumstances.[167]

Notice how reality is constructed by the individual, since there is no truth, just interpretations by different people and cultures. If the woman does not want the fetus, then no crime has been perpetrated on the baby at the abortion clinic; after all, it is simply tissue. But if the mother wants the child, then the criminal has killed two people; the tissue was a person with rights. This is an example of the contradictions we live with in this era, a reality being subjectively constructed by human thought, not objective reality. This has great appeal to our individual desire to be free and autonomous, setting the rules for ourselves.

# Tolerance— Old and New Definitions

Yet to speak about these issues, whether it is the evils of abortion or the truthfulness of Christianity, is to run counter to the postmodern mind-set. Nothing offends people today more than to claim to have the truth. Since there is no truth, no one can claim to have it. It is diametrically opposed to the very core tenets of postmodernism. And that's why postmodernists call for tolerance.

Today, there are actually two working definitions of tolerance. It would serve you well to determine which definition is in use when people use this term. You can accomplish that by simply asking for their definition. The old definition is "recognizing others' beliefs without sharing them." For example, someone is a Christian, and someone is a Muslim. You understand what they believe, but you don't share their particular view, so you live and let live. Sometimes this is called "negative" tolerance.

> **The old definition of tolerance is recognizing others' beliefs without sharing them.**

However, "positive" tolerance (the new definition) is recognizing that everyone's beliefs are equal, and no truth claim is greater than another. All beliefs are tolerated because none can actually be the truth. Remember, every worldview begins with an assumption; postmodernism says there is no God. It further states that there is no truth, just interpretations by different people and cultures, and all these interpretations are equally valid. So any person or group that claims to have the truth is judging the beliefs of others and therefore is intolerant. By claiming to have the truth they are trying to dominate other cultures.[168] Those who are intolerant will suffer consequences—sensitivity classes, a mark on their permanent record, loss of class credit, or employment opportunities surrendered. Yet examples occur daily of people standing up for the truth and willingly suffering for it. Thankfully, groups such as The Alliance Defense Fund offer help. ADF is a Christian organization that defends and protects the right to hear and speak the truth in communities across America.

> **The new tolerance is that everyone's beliefs are equal; no truth claim is greater than another.**

But in the midst of the desire to be tolerant, did you notice the double standard? If all beliefs are equal, then people should tolerate intolerance. If Christians have their truth, no one can judge them for it just because they say it is the truth. Chuck Colson states it this way:

But the creed for the new god of tolerance is that knowing truth is impossible. So everyone is free to think and act as he likes, with one exception: those who have the audacity to believe that they know the truth, particularly if they think God has revealed it to them, are not tolerated. The result is that those who crowned the new god of tolerance have become the absolute arbiters of culture.[169]

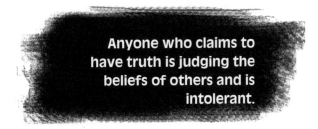

Anyone who claims to have truth is judging the beliefs of others and is intolerant.

But there are other consequences to this postmodern thinking as well.

# Postmodern Consequences:
## Personal Responses to Postmodern Times

First, we need to understand the times and be aware of the various mind-sets around us. 1 Chronicles 12:32 mentions men who joined David to fight with him: "Men who had understanding of the times, to know what Israel ought to do." In similar fashion, we should be educated in the worldviews of the day so that we might be able to witness effectively. Christian apologist Ravi Zacharias says that understanding what we believe and what other people believe is key to this century.[170] Reading this book is one step in the right direction. There's more to know, but it's a start.

**We need to understand the times and be aware of various mind-sets around us.**

Second, we need to develop convictions. A conviction is a belief that we are thoroughly convinced is true and for which we are willing to take a stand. We need to grow from just believing the Christian faith to being thoroughly convinced it is true. We hope this book has helped convince you if there were doubts in your mind regarding the trustworthiness of the Bible or the Christian message. Paul encouraged Timothy to remain in what he had discovered to be true in 2 Timothy 3:14–15.

> But as for you, continue in what you have learned and have firmly believed, knowing from whom you learned it and how from childhood you have been acquainted with the sacred writings, which are able to make you wise for salvation through faith in Christ Jesus.

**We need to grow from just believing Christianity to being thoroughly convinced it is true.**

Third, we should pursue the truth. Not only is Jesus the truth (John 14:6), but the Bible is the truth as well (John 17:17). We need to study and know the Bible, along with apologetics, because we are sent to the world to evangelize. In a postmodern world of no truth, we need all the truth we can get! Jesus prayed for His apostles in John 17:15–18:

I do not ask that You take them out of the world, but that You keep them from the evil one. They are not of the world, just as I am not of the world. Sanctify them in the truth; Your word is truth. As You sent me into the world, so I have sent them into the world.

> **We need to study and know the Bible, along with apologetics, because we are sent to the world.**

Fourth and finally, we are to love our enemies, which is the true mark of a Christian. It is inevitable people will disagree with you; some will call you intolerant or narrow-minded in this postmodern culture. Instead of name-calling or fighting back, Christ calls us to imitate Him and make a lasting impression on people. Jesus told His disciples, "Love your enemies and pray for those who persecute you" (Matthew 5:44). Sometimes how you act will have an even greater impact than what you say.

> **We are to love our enemies, which is the true mark of a Christian.**

# Public Responses in Postmodern Times

We *are* called to witness as we have noted from these previous verses. So how can we do this effectively today? Ravi Zacharias gives us some pointers for dealing with postmodern public situations.[171] In order to present the Gospel today, instead of opening the Bible first, ask questions of your audience. Then illustrate your point with examples. Finally bring the truth, the Bible, to the discussion. The reason for leading with questions *first*, following with examples for illustration, and finishing with the Bible *last* is because only about one-third of the American adult population believes that the Bible is the actual Word of God and is to be taken, word-for-word, as true. We addressed this fact in an earlier chapter on the Bible. We have to know our audience—what they believe and don't believe.

> **Ask questions of your audience. Illustrate your point with examples. Then open the Bible.**

For example, if you've done your homework and know the postmodern tenets, ask people if they agree with pluralism—that everyone is right, since there is no truth. If this is correct, it leads to contradictions and no reason. Illustrate your point with a discussion about the person of Jesus Christ to both Muslims and Christians. If they are both right, how can Jesus be merely a prophet to the Muslims and the Son of God and Savior of the world to the Christians? To hold on to both views is a contradiction. Follow up with the Bible, applying what Jesus said in John 14:6, "I am the way, and the truth, and the life. No one comes to the Father except through Me." Remember, if people say that's just your truth, point out the contradictions in their postmodern thinking. The very idea that there is no truth undercuts itself. "There is no truth" becomes a truth statement.

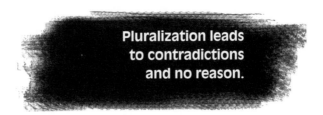

> Pluralization leads to contradictions and no reason.

Take another witnessing situation. In the name of the new tolerance, people today say you can believe whatever you want; just don't let it affect public life and policy. We don't want to offend anyone. This is called privatization, when individuals separate their private and public life. It leads to no meaning—what good is their religion if they don't use it? To illustrate your point, consider this example. Say you're stranded in a strange part of town all alone with no cell phone. Five Christians approached you, discussing the great Bible study they just finished. What would you expect them to do? Wouldn't you expect them to help? Wouldn't you expect them to live their private faith in a public way by helping you? On the other hand, if they walked past and left you stranded, or worse yet, attacked you, you'd be sickened by their hypocrisy. As James 2:26 says, "Faith apart from works is dead." We expect private faith to come out in public life. From the abolition of slavery to the founding of schools and hospitals, Christianity has a rich history of making society better.

> Privatization, when individuals separate their private and public life, leads to no meaning.

Postmodernism proves to be complex, contradictory, and constantly changing.[172] Thank God He does not change: "Jesus Christ is the same yesterday and today and forever" (Hebrews 13:8). In the midst of our earthly confusion, the Bible is dependable and God is faithful, as we have seen from earlier chapters. The Christian worldview map can be used to navigate anywhere, anytime, and with anyone. It applies to all of us. It is universal. It is a meta-narrative, an overarching explanation of all things, and the truth. Let's conclude this book with an examination of this truth, which is available for all people, at all times, and in all places. It is a truth that meets our deepest needs.

# Chapter 13

## How Can We Witness Effectively Today?

### The "Two-Story Truth" of Faith and Reason

In the last chapter, we saw how in the postmodern world in which we live there is no universal Truth (capital *T*); there are only "truths" (small *t*) that are particular to a society and limited to individual perception. On the other hand, Christianity offers a "comprehensive, unified worldview that addresses all of life and reality. It is not just religious truth but total truth."[173] As we have seen, God gives the big answers to the big questions we all have: how the orderly universe came to be in existence through creation, how evil and suffering entered the world through Adam and Eve's rebellion, and how God dealt with humanity's sin through His Son, Jesus Christ. Moreover, the Bible explains why we were created, what happens when we die, and how we can live as His people who have been saved by grace through faith in Jesus as Savior. The Bible is God's Word, a reliable book that has been accurately handed down without essential loss from generation to generation. The accounts, from the flood to Jesus' life, can be geologically, geographically, historically, and archaeologically verified. It is not just true for me as in postmodernism, but it is true for all of us.

Yet the very concept of a universal truth is not only rejected by postmodernism, but also religion itself is consigned to irrelevance as we noted at the end of the last chapter. Through privatization, individuals separate their private and public life by living in what Christian philosopher Francis Schaeffer described as a "two-story truth." Imagine a building with two levels. The lower level of the two-story truth is the realm of reason, an area of objective, scientific knowledge and facts. On this level, the battle cry is "True for all" because no one can argue with rational, verifiable facts, like two plus two equals four. However, on the upper level of the two-story truth is the realm of faith, an area of subjective, personal preferences and values. Here the statement is *"That's true for you, but not for me." Believing Jesus is Savior and Lord is just a truth for my personal life; it is not objectively true or verifiable.*[174]

> **Two-story truth: the realms of reason and objective facts, with faith and subjective values.**

What makes witnessing so difficult in today's postmodern age is because of this dichotomy, or two-story truth, religion is respected but irrelevant. It's just your own personal belief; it's not anything we can use in the public arena, because there are no universal truths for all people. Regarding issues such as abortion, embryonic stem cells, and homosexuality, the lower level of reason in the two-story truth has much to say. That's the area of science and objective facts. But not so for the upper story of faith—it's just subjective preferences and feelings. Historian of religion Martin Marty says this is "the first time in history where Christianity has been boxed into the private sphere and has largely stopped speaking to the public sphere."[175]

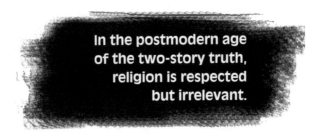

In the postmodern age of the two-story truth, religion is respected but irrelevant.

If Christians surrender to this temptation to stop speaking, keeping "the Christian truth" to oneself in the private areas of our lives or in our churches, what good is our religion? We discussed this in the previous chapter. Furthermore, this separating of private and public lives is unique to the West and is the greatest barrier to the power of the Word for our culture.[176] "Keep your religion to yourself" is based on the idea that your position on a public issue is not an objective truth but is a subjective bias. How do we witness effectively in these days when confronted with this mind-set?

# Effective Witnessing

What we need to remember is one of the principles from the beginning of the book: all worldviews begin with assumptions. Nancy Pearcey states it like this:

> Others promote their own views as unbiased and rational, suitable for the public square, while denouncing religious views as biased or prejudiced. This tactic has often cowed Christians into being defensive about our faith. . . . The mistake lies in thinking there is such a thing as theories that are unbiased or neutral, unaffected by any religious or philosophical assumptions.[177]

When we grasp that all worldviews start with assumptions, and we bring that out into the open with people, it aids in the discussion, because now all can think through presuppositions that were absorbed previously without much discernment.

**Remember: all worldviews begin with assumptions.**

Take, for example, the concept of God's existence: He either is or isn't. These assumptions lead you down two dramatically different paths. Or take the concept that there is no truth. How do you know? Isn't that a truth statement in and of itself? Helping people recognize assumptions is one key in witnessing.

Another key in witnessing is understanding the proper place of apologetics. Knowledge of facts doesn't bring salvation; Jesus does, by the power of the Holy Spirit, when we're convicted of our sin and convinced He's our Savior. The facts brought forward in this book are meant to show the reliability of the Bible and the truthfulness of the message in it. However, arguments in this book defending the Scriptures and the historicity of Jesus will work only when nonbelievers still adhere to the concepts of true and false. In our postmodern culture, many don't buy into those concepts.

**In postmodern culture, many don't buy into true and false; you see if something works.**

There is no truth, just beliefs that are products of human subjectivity. You don't test whether something is objectively true; you see if it works or has beneficial effects in the lives of people who believe it. For example, does it make them happy or give them meaning? That's what makes something true—if it is pragmatic.[178] Josh McDowell rightly points out, "This generation, as a rule, is not asking, 'Is it true?' but rather 'Does it work?' "[179] Others point out being orthodox no longer matters. Doing what works for you is what matters. If this means going to Catholic Mass on your way to yoga and a Buddhist retreat center, good for you.[180] So while being a Catholic-Buddhist may seem contradictory on a logical level, it is not so for the postmodernist.

Yet here is where we must help people think through their beliefs before we show the truth of the Bible as we discussed previously. If all beliefs are not really true, but only useful, then this postmodern concept itself is not true either. A statement that undercuts itself is self-defeating or self-referentially absurd.[181] An example of this is a married bachelor—there's no such thing! When postmodernists claim there's no truth, just whatever works for you, why should the rest of us pay any attention? Their own claim fits in the category of no truth.

> **If there's no truth, just evolved beliefs, why should we pay attention to postmodernism?**

In addition, we can point out since there's no truth, there's no measure to gauge whether what works is good or bad, right or wrong. Is lying bad? Is cheating good? If the measure for truth is whether something simply works, then "immediate workability" will lead to instant gratification and temporary fixes that are not necessarily moral.[182] They simply achieve what a person wants. Worse yet, it often leads to whatever the most powerful people want, and others will suffer for it.

> **If there's no truth, there's no measure to gauge whether what works is good or bad.**

Furthermore, beliefs can be useful and *false*; for instance, take the belief in Santa Claus. Telling children to be good so Santa will bring presents on Christmas has a certain usefulness to it, but there is no one actually coming down the chimney. Another example of a false belief being useful is the political spin explaining the first Gulf War in 1991. One postmodernist went so far as to claim that the Gulf War was not real, but merely simulated for CNN.[183] The fact that real people were dying never factored into the equation. It really *does* matter if a belief is true, not just how it makes you feel.

This leads to another key for witnessing in this age—does the worldview match reality? Returning to the two-story truth, the splitting of faith and reason: it does not explain life as we know it. From the lower story of reason we are told we are evolved animals in a random, purposeless world. We are bombarded with evolution from all sides—television, movies, education, museums, and the like. Yet, in the upper story of faith, we are also told we should act with dignity and respect, treating others fairly, being gracious and kind. Why? From where did these thoughts and emotions evolve? Why should we follow those commands if there's no God and all religions and, for that matter, all other ideas are just man-made stories that societies have conditioned their people to accept? "This is the tragedy of the postmodern age: The things that matter most in life—freedom and dignity, meaning and significance—have been reduced to nothing but useful fictions. Wishful thinking. Irrational mysticism."[184]

> **The two-story truth, the splitting of faith and reason, does not explain life as we know it.**

This thinking creates tension in people. Is there a God? The assumption is no. If we are evolved animals, then why should I treat others well? Why shouldn't I lie, cheat, and steal to get what I want? This leads to confusion and no meaning to life. "It produces an inner division between what people *think they know* and what they desperately *want to believe* (that our lives have purpose and meaning)."[185] We turn to money, drugs, relationships, or anything else to give us purpose, because there is no truth—just whatever we subjectively believe. Yet that's not what we experience. We see designed beauty in the universe, feel guilt when we do wrong, and hear about the love of God in Christ Jesus. And that's the best way to witness—point out the distinction between what people *believe* and what they *know* experientially.

> **Point out the distinction between what people believe and what they know experientially.**

The best witnessing comes when you allow a person to examine his or her worldview's starting assumption, then look at the philosophy of what's real and the person's ethics on how to live. Then ask him to check his worldview with the real world. Does he believe there's *no God? How does he know?* Does he believe in evolution? Why is there order from a chaotic explosion in the big bang theory? How did life come from lifelessness when the law of biogenesis says it cannot? Is there any wrong behavior, or are there limits to what we can do? Who decides? Why can they decide? Why do all cultures have laws? When a *worldview* points in one direction while *life experience* points in another, then one cannot live on the basis of the professed worldview. It is not a "workable guide for navigating the world."[186] The map is useless.

As we proceed, we need to show how Christianity is unified truth on both levels of faith and reason. It works in everyday life, yet fits the facts of objective truth that can be verified. Christianity satisfies both intellectually and spiritually. In the two-story truth, the lower level of reason is satisfied because Christianity stands up to rational and historical testing. The majority of the book has dealt with those issues. In the upper level of faith, it is fulfilling our deepest spiritual needs. Am I loved? Am I forgiven? Does my life have meaning? The answers are yes in Jesus! Nancy Pearcey said it best:

> What Christianity offers is a unified, integrated truth that stands in complete contrast to the two-level concept of truth in the secular world. . . . Christianity rests on historical events that at the same time express the most exalted spiritual meanings. There is no division into contradictory, opposing levels of truth—and therefore no division in a person's inner life either. Christianity fulfills both our reason and our spiritual yearnings. This is truly good news. We can offer the world a unified truth that is intellectually satisfying, while at the same time it meets our deepest hunger for beauty and meaning. . . . It is true not about only a limited aspect of reality but about total reality. It is total truth.[187]

**Christianity is truth on both levels, satisfying spiritual needs while standing up to tests.**

# A Christian Worldview

In summary, this total truth, a Christian worldview, is a biblically informed perspective on the world. Christianity starts with the presupposition that God exists due to the order in the universe and the moral order in the world. God reveals Himself generally through nature and more specifically through His Word. He who is absolute and unchanging is the source of all truth. Even though God created a perfect world, humans rebelled in sin against Him and ruined it.

To restore the relationship with God, Jesus Christ came to save sinners. Jesus told Zacchaeus the tax collector, "For the Son of Man came to seek and to save the lost" (Luke 19:10). But Jesus also came to testify to the truth. While on trial before Pontius Pilate, Jesus said, "You say that I am a king. For this purpose I was born and for this purpose I have come into the world—to bear witness to the truth. Everyone who is of the truth listens to My voice" (John 18:37). There is either the truth or the lies. Which side will you be on?

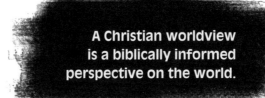

**A Christian worldview is a biblically informed perspective on the world.**

The hard truth is all people are sinners—everyone has broken God's Law and deserves nothing but punishment for evil. People feel guilty over the bad things they've done because those "who do not have the law, by nature do what the law requires, they are a law to themselves, even though they do not have the law" (Romans 2:14). Reading God's Word, the Bible, will reveal the specific laws they've broken, adding more guilt because "by works of the law no human being will be justified in His sight, since through the law comes knowledge of sin" (Romans 3:20). However, continuing to read God's Word will not only show people their sin, it will also show them their Savior.

> But now the righteousness of God has been manifested apart from the law, although the Law and the Prophets bear witness to it—the righteousness of God through faith in Jesus Christ for all who believe. For there is no distinction: for all have sinned and fall short of the glory of God, and are justified by His grace as a gift, through the redemption that is in Christ Jesus. Romans 3:21–24

> The Law shows us
> our sin; the Gospel
> shows us our Savior.

So Christianity is what Nancy Pearcey calls *Total Truth*—it is truth about all reality, for all people and all times. And it is the map to navigate the world effectively so we live in line with God's intentions when it comes to ethics and our behavior. God exists and made everything. In love, He redeemed humanity through Jesus' death and resurrection after we rebelled. He knows what is best for our lives because He made us. But if Adam and Eve rejecting God and His perfect world weren't bad enough, today we continue to reject His Son and the plan to bring perfection to our sinful souls. The apostle Paul says, "They exchanged the truth about God for a lie and worshiped and served the creature rather than the Creator" (Romans 1:25). Just like Adam and Eve, we reject God and His plan, thinking our way is better, and we exchange the true worldview for false ones.

> Christianity is total truth—
> truth about all reality, for
> all people and all times.

## Biblical Discernment

Unfortunately, many today confess Jesus as Savior, yet don't even realize how other worldviews have affected their own thinking. Whether it is postmodernism or secular humanism or whatever "ism" you want to name, Christians using other worldviews will be unconsciously shaped by their assumptions. Just as wearing someone else's glasses affects your vision, so using another's worldview affects your perception of reality.[188] That's why the Bible tells us to be critical thinkers, using the Bible as the source and norm of measuring truth. We are to examine all thoughts thoroughly and test them with the Bible, rather than soaking them in like a sponge without discernment. Paul commands us to "test everything; hold fast what is good. Abstain from every form of evil" (1 Thessalonians 5:21–22). In 2 Corinthians 10:5, Paul writes, "We destroy arguments and every lofty opinion raised against the knowledge of God, and take every thought captive to obey Christ." Don't check your brains at the classroom door or when you read something—seize those thoughts, taking them captive to the Lord of truth and His Word, and check them against Scripture. For example, if the discussion is on whether people are basically good or not, ask if this is a biblical perspective on the nature of man. The Bible, as well as our everyday experience, reveals that humans are not basically good or neutral; we are sinful, which explains the terrible decisions people make each day.

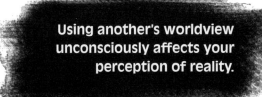

Using another's worldview unconsciously affects your perception of reality.

These other worldviews are all around us, just as they were in Paul's day. That's why he told the Christians in Colossae, "See to it that no one takes you captive by philosophy and empty deceit, according to human tradition, according to the elemental spirits of the world, and not according to Christ" (Colossians 2:8). There are teachings based on human concepts that don't ultimately satisfy the intellectual and spiritual hunger that all people have. Only Christ, "in whom are hidden all the treasures of wisdom and knowledge" (Colossians 2:3), can fulfill those needs. So Paul warned his readers not to be taken captive by lying philosophies. If we don't analyze worldviews—the starting assumption, the philosophy of what's real regarding the supernatural and natural realms, and the ethical standards of how to live—then we will buy the lies people are selling. Once we've bought the lies, and our mind thinks a certain way, our actions continue down that path. That's why we need to be enlightened by God's truth through the power of the Holy Spirit to free us from this captivity. Paul wrote in Romans 12:2, "Do not be conformed to this world, but be transformed by the renewal of your mind, that by testing you may discern what is the will of God, what is good and acceptable and perfect." Once God reveals the truth to you and transforms your mind by renewing it with the light of truth, then you live in accordance with His Word, testing with the Bible what is right and true as opposed to what is not.

> **Examine all thoughts and test them with the Word; let God change your mind with His Word.**

## The Need for Understanding Worldviews

Many of the concepts encircling the globe today are opposed to God's Word. Worldviews give birth to ideas, and the world revolves around these concepts, such as macro-evolution, jihad, infanticide, or the new tolerance.[189] Obviously, these ideas have consequences. From a Christian worldview, sinful people produce bad ideas leading to negative consequences. This explains the reality of life as we experience it every day. Yet Christians need to understand what others believe and why. Nancy Pearcey writes:

> Before they leave home, they should be well acquainted with all the "isms" they will encounter, from Marxism to Darwinism to postmodernism. It is best for young believers to hear about these ideas first from trusted parents, pastors, and youth leaders, who can train them in strategies for analyzing competing ideologies.[190]

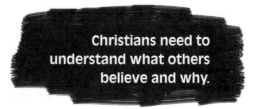

**Christians need to understand what others believe and why.**

Why bother studying various worldviews? Don't we have enough of the Bible to study? We study the Bible as well as these other worldviews because souls, as well as institutions, are at stake. Christians need to make a difference; we are sent into the world with the Great Commission: "Go therefore and make disciples of all nations, baptizing them in the name of the Father and of the Son and of the Holy Spirit, teaching them to observe all that I have commanded you" (Matthew 28:19–20). People's lives, way of life, and eternal souls are on the line—that's why we study what others believe. The love of Christ motivates us to talk.

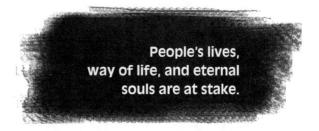

**People's lives, way of life, and eternal souls are at stake.**

Furthermore, our understanding of their worldview enhances the way we witness. "As Christians we are called to be missionaries to our world, and that means learning the language and thought-forms of the people we want to reach."[191] As discussed earlier, the best way to make a window for witnessing is by showing the conflict of what people believe but know experientially. When someone says people are basically good, you ask if they lock their door at night. They shouldn't if people are good—what do they have to fear? When someone says we're evolved animals, you ask if they are upset when a murder takes place. They shouldn't be if we're animals—creatures kill each other every day in the wild. People's inconsistency, when their worldview points in one direction while their life experience points in another, reveals that their map doesn't work. But you have to do your homework first and know where people are coming from.

> **Do your homework first and know where people are coming from.**

That's why Paul was bothered about the unbelievers in Athens and why he did something about it. He had done his homework and knew the worldview of the people.

> **Now while Paul was waiting for them at Athens, his spirit was provoked within him as he saw that the city was full of idols. So he reasoned in the synagogue with the Jews and the devout persons, and in the marketplace every day with those who happened to be there. Acts 17:16–17**

Paul became distraught over these unbelievers in Athens so he reasoned with them in the synagogue and market on a daily basis. To what end? So that he might be known as the smartest man in Athens? No, not at all. Paul shares his motivation for witnessing in 1 Corinthians 9:22–23, "To the weak I became weak, that I might win the weak. I have become all things to all people, that by all means I might save some. I do it all for the sake of the Gospel, that I may share with them in its blessings."

Paul knew the truth—the eternal stakes on the line. Paul also knew the heart of God; he said it best in 1 Timothy 2:3–4: "This is good, and it is pleasing in the sight of God our Savior, who desires all people to be saved and to come to the knowledge of the truth." The truth is this: God made us, we sinned, and we will be cut off from Him eternally because of our sin unless we receive the salvation He provides through Jesus Christ by grace through faith. Remember, Jesus said, "For this purpose I was born and for this purpose I have come into the world—to bear witness to the truth. Everyone who is of the truth listens to My voice" (John 18:37). That's why Jesus said, "I am the way, and the truth, and the life. No one comes to the Father except through Me" (John 14:6).

God has the big answers to life's big questions, providing us with the map to lead us to eternal life in heaven through faith in

Jesus' salvation, while also leading us in everyday life so we live in accordance with God's will. It is my prayer that you know Jesus, the way, the truth, and the life.

# Endnotes

1   George Barna, *The State of the Church: 2002* (Ventura, CA: Issachar Resources, 2002), p. 110.

2   Christian Smith, *Soul Searching: The Religious and Spiritual Lives of American Teenagers* (New York: Oxford University Press, 2005), p. 89.

3   George Barna, *Third Millennium Teens* (Ventura, CA: Barna Research Group, Ltd., 1999), p. 47.

4   Josh McDowell, *The Last Christian Generation* (Holiday, FL: Green Key Books, 2006), pp. 41–49.

5   Ibid., pp. 57–65.

6   Josh McDowell, *The New Evidence That Demands a Verdict* (Nashville, TN: Thomas Nelson Publishers, 1999), p. xl.

7   David Noebel, *Understanding the Times* (Manitou Springs, CO: Summit Press, 2006), p. 16.

8   John MacArthur, "What's Your Worldview?" *Answers*, July–September 2006, pp. 12–13.

9   Barna, *Third Millennium Teens*, p. 51.

10   Eric Gorski, "Survey shows growing religious tolerance," *The Milwaukee Journal Sentinel*, June 25, 2008.

11   MacArthur, pp. 12–13.

12   Scott Todd, "A view from Kansas on that evolution debate," *Nature*, September 30, 1999, p. 423.

13   Nancy Pearcey, *Total Truth: Liberating Christianity from Its Cultural Captivity,* © 2004. Used by permission of Crossways Books, a publishing ministry of Good News Publishers, Wheaton, IL 60187, www.crossways.org, p. 23.

14   Carl Sagan, *Cosmos* (New York: Random House, 1980), p. 4.

15   Pearcey, p. 23.

16   "Students Protest Princeton Professor Who Advocates Infanticide." Available online at http://www.euthanasia.com/prince.html (accessed January 2009).

17   Noebel, p. 14.

18   *The Truth Project*. Directed by Simon Scionka, with Del Tackett. Focus on the Family, 2006.

19   Pearcey, p. 42.

20   Noebel, p. 17.

21   *American Heritage Dictionary*. William Morris, ed. (Boston: Houghton Mifflin Company, 1978).

22    Noebel, p. 17.

23    *The Truth Project.*

24    Pearcey, p. 314.

25    Sagan, p. 4.

26    Paul Kurtz, *Humanist Manifestos I and II* (Amherst, NY: Prometheus Books, 1973), p. 8.

27    "What does entropy have to do with the Bible and refuting compromise regarding the Bible?" http://www.answersingenesis.org/e-mail/archive/ AnswersWeekly/2007/0602.asp (accessed February 2009).

28    Max Jammer, *Einstein and Religion* (Princeton, NJ: Princeton University Press, 1999), p. 48.

29    Sharon Begley, "Science Finds God," *Newsweek*, July 20, 1998, p. 48.

30    *Frontiers of Modern Biology on Theories of Origin of Life* (New York: Houghton Mifflin, 1972), p. 187.

31    *X-Men.* Directed by Bryan Singer, with Patrick Stewart. 20th Century Fox, 2000.

32    Michael Behe, *The Edge of Evolution* (New York: Free Press, 2007), pp. 141–42.

33    John Sanford, *Genetic Entropy and the Mystery of the Genome* (Lima, NY: Ivan Press, 2005), p. 40.

34    Tom Bethel, *The Politically Incorrect Guide to Science* (Washington DC: Regnery Publishing, 2005), p. 218.

35    Begley, p. 48.

36    *In 6 Days,* http://www.answersingenesis.org/home/area/isd/Sarfati.asp (accessed June 2009).

37    "Evidence for a Young World," http://www.answersingenesis.org/docs/4005.asp (accessed July 2009).

38    Ken Ham, *The New Answers Book 2* (Green Forest, AR: Master Books, 2008), p. 241.

39    "How old is the earth?" http://www.answersingenesis.org/articles/2007/05/30/ how-old-is-earth (accessed June 2009).

40    "Noah's Flood: Where did the water come from?" http://www.answersingenesis. org/home/area/tools/flood-waters.asp (accessed July 2009).

41    *In 6 Days.*

42    Alan Moore, *Watchmen,* vol. 6 (New York: DC Comics, 1987), p. 28.

43    Pearcey, p. 48.

44    Ibid., p. 55.

45    Charles Colson, *The Faith* (Grand Rapids, MI: Zondervan, 2008), p. 77.

46  John Fountain, "Taking aim at evil," *Milwaukee Journal Sentinel,* December 3, 2000.

47  Pearcey, p. 55.

48  Robert Hutchinson, *The Politically Incorrect Guide to the Bible* (Washington DC: Regnery, 2007), p. 193.

49  Ibid., p. 14.

50  David van Biema, "God vs. Science," *Time*, November 5, 2006, http://www.time.com/time/magazine/article/0,9171,555132,00.html.

51  Sharon Begley, "Don't Blame the Caveman," *Newsweek*, June 29, 2009, p. 53.

52  Ibid., p. 54.

53  Pearcey, p. 218.

54  "One-third of Americans believe the Bible is literally true," http://www.gallup.com/poll/27682/OneThird-Americans-Believe-Bible-Literally-True.aspx (accessed July 2009).

55  Edward Koehler, *A Summary of Christian Doctrine* (St. Louis: Concordia Publishing House, 1971), p. 5.

56  McDowell, *The New Evidence That Demands a Verdict*, pp. 17–18.

57  Ibid., p. 79.

58  Ibid., p. 76.

59  http://www.isionline.org/pdfs/Religion%20Profiles/Word%20of%20God%20 2004.PDF (accessed July 2009).

60  Ibid., p. 35.

61  Ibid., p. 38.

62  Archer, Gleason L., *Encyclopedia of Bible Difficulties* (Grand Rapids, MI: Zondervan, 1982), p. 12.

63  Dan Brown, *The Da Vinci Code* (New York: Anchor Books, 2003), p. 251.

64  McDowell, *The New Evidence That Demands a Verdict*, p. 21.

65  Ibid., p. 26.

66  Ibid., p. 22.

67  Martin Franzmann, *The Word of the Lord Grows* (St. Louis: Concordia Publishing House, 1961), pp. 288–89.

68  Ibid., pp. 288, 290.

69  Ibid., pp. 287, 292.

70  McDowell, *The New Evidence That Demands a Verdict,* pp. 29, 31–32.

71  Duane Gisch, *Dinosaurs by Design* (Green Forest, AR: Master Books, 1992), pp. 74–75.

72  Pam Sheppard, "Tongue Twisting Tales," *Answers*, April–May 2008, pp. 56–57.

73  Ken Ham, *The New Answers Book* (Green Forest, AR: Master Books, 2006), p. 133.

74  Ibid., p. 137.

75  Ibid., p. 135.

76  Ibid., p. 135.

77  "Noah's Flood: Where did the water come from?" http://www.answersingenesis. org/home/area/tools/flood-waters.asp (accessed July 2009).

78  Andrew Snelling, "Catastrophic Breakup," *Answers*, April–June 2007, pp. 44–48.

79  John Whitcomb, *The World That Perished* (Grand Rapids, MI: Baker Book House, 1988), p. 25.

80  Ham, *The New Answers Book*, p. 130.

81  Ibid., p. 129.

82  Ibid., p. 130.

83  Tim Lovett, "Thinking Outside the Box," *Answers*, April–June 2007, p. 27.

84  Whitcomb, p. 24.

85  Ibid., p. 130.

86  Ham, *The New Answers Book*, p. 138.

87  Ibid., p. 225.

88  Ibid., p. 229.

89  John Whitcomb and Henry Morris, *The Genesis Flood: The Biblical Record and Its Scientific Implications* (Phillipsburg, NJ: Presbyterian and Reformed Publishing, 1961), p. 86.

90  Ham, *The New Answers Book*, p. 145.

91  Andrew Snelling, "High and Dry Sea Creatures," *Answers*, January–March 2008, pp. 92–95.

92  Whitcomb, p. 44.

93  "What is the most compelling scientific evidence of a young earth?" http:// www.answersingenesis.org/home/area/feedback/2006/0303.asp (accessed July 2009)

94  Andrew Snelling, "The World's a Graveyard," *Answers*, April–June 2008, pp. 76–79.

95  Andrew Snelling, "Transcontinental Rock Layers," *Answers*, July–September 2008, pp. 80–83.

96  Andrew Snelling, "No Slow and Gradual Erosion," *Answers*, January–March 2009, pp. 96–99.

97  Whitcomb, p. 75.

98   "What is the most compelling scientific evidence of a young earth?" http://
     www.answersingenesis.org/home/area/feedback/2006/0303.asp (accessed July
     2009).

99   Andrew Snelling, "Rock Layers Folded not Fractured," *Answers*, April–June
     2009, pp. 80–83.

100  *The Incredible Discovery of Noah's Ark*, Dir. Henning Schellerup, Grizzly Adams
     Productions, 1993.

101  Ibid., and "Eyewitness List," http://www.noahsarksearch.com (accessed July
     2009).

102  John Morris, "Has Noah's Ark Been Found?" *Answers*, April–June 2007, pp.
     70–73.

103  Ham, *The New Answers Book*, p. 158.

104  Whitcomb, p. 80.

105  Ibid., p. 83.

106  Ham, *The New Answers Book*, p. 167.

107  Michael Oard, "Setting the Stage for an Ice Age," *Answers*, April–June 2007, pp.
     59–61.

108  Ham, *The New Answers Book 2*, p. 132.

109  Ham, *The New Answers Book*, p. 170.

110  Ham, *The New Answers Book 2*, p. 118.

111  Ham, *The New Answers Book*, pp. 161–62.

112  "Messages on stone," http://www.answersingenesis.org/creation/v19/i2/stone.
     asp (accessed July 2009).

113  "Are dinosaurs alive today?" http://www.answersingenesis.org/creation/v15/
     i4/dinosaurs.asp (accessed July 2009).

114  "A living dinosaur?" *Creation*, December 2000–February 2001, p. 56.

115  Ham, *The New Answers Book* p. 159.

116  Ibid., p. 160.

117  Ibid., p. 159.

118  McDowell, *The New Evidence That Demands a Verdict*, p. 89.

119  Ibid., p. 95.

120  "Solomon," http://home.paonline.com/ahanna/HTML/SOLOMON.htm
     (cited July 2009).

121  McDowell, *The New Evidence That Demands a Verdict*, p. 63.

122  The Mishnah tractate, *Sanhedrin* 43a.

123  Shlomo Pines, "An Arabic Version of the Testamonium Flavianum and Its
     Implications," (Jerusalem: The Israel Acadaemy of Science and Humanities,

1971), Reproduced by permission.

124   "Josephus and Jesus," http://www.4truth.net/site/c.hiKXLbPNLrF/ b.2902067/k.C923/Josephus_and_Jesus.htm (accessed July 2009).

125   Josephus, *Jewish Antiquities* 20:200.

126   Julius Africanus, *Chronography*, 18.1.

127   Bruce, F. F. , *The New Testament Documents: Are They Reliable?* Fifth revised edition. (Downers Grove, IL: Inter-Varsity Press, 1972), p. 113..

128   Julius Africanus, *Chronography*, 18.1.

129   Tacitus, *Annals* XV, 44.

130   Lucian, *The Death of Peregrine*, 11–13.

131   Suetonius, *Lives of the Caesars*, 26.2.

132   Tacitus, *Annals* XV, 44.

133   Pliny the Younger, Epistles X, 96.

134   Ibid.

135"Mara bar Serapion on the wise king of the Jews," www.textexcavation.com/ marabarserapiontestimonium.html (accessed July 2009).

136   McDowell, *The New Evidence That Demands a Verdict*, p. 136.

137   Ibid., p. 205.

138   Lee Strobel, *The Case for Christ* (Grand Rapids, MI: Zondervan, 1998), p. 192.

139   McDowell, *The New Evidence That Demands a Verdict*, p. 259.

140   Ibid., p. 261.

141   Strobel, p. 198.

142   Gerard Stanley and Kent Burreson, *He Was Crucified: Reflections on the Passion of Christ* (St. Louis: Concordia Publishing House, 2009) p. 150.

143   McDowell, *The New Evidence That Demands a Verdict*, p. 266.

144   Ibid., p. 267.

145   Ibid., p. 264.

146   Strobel, *The Case for Christ*, p. 239.

147   Ibid., p. 238.

148   Ibid., p. 218.

149   Merrill Unger, *Unger's Bible Dictionary* (Chicago: Moody Press, 1966) p. 138.

150   "The Word—Why trust the Bible?" http://www.slideshare.net/schumacr/the-word- why-trust-the-bible-1638014 (accessed August 2009).

151   C. S. Lewis, *Mere Christianity* (New York: HarperSanFrancisco, 1952), p. 52. Copyright © C.S. Lewis Pte. Ltd. 1942, 1943, 1944, 1952. Extract reprinted by permission..

152   Josephus, *Jewish Antiquities* 18:63.

153   "Major religions of the world ranked by number of adherents," http://www.adherents.com/Religions_By_Adherents.html (accessed August 2009).

154   *American Heritage Dictionary*. William Morris, ed. (Boston: Houghton Mifflin Company, 1978).

155   John Stonestreet, "Understanding Postmodernism," *Understanding the Times Curriculum* (Manitou Springs, CO: Summit Press, 2006), pp. 63–66.

156   McDowell, *The Last Christian Generation*, p. 43.

157   Noebel, p. 121.

158   Ibid., p. 120.

159   McDowell, *The Last Christian Generation*, p. 43.

160   Paul Kurtz, *Humanist Manifesto 2000* (Amherst, NY: Prometheus Books, 1973), p. 22.

161   Pearcey, p. 243.

162   Noebel, p. 120.

163   Ibid., pp. 120–21.

164   "Postmodernism and the Christian Life," http://www.boundless.org/features/a0000917.html (accessed August 2009).

165   Edward Koehler, *A Summary of Christian Doctrine* (St. Louis: Concordia Publishing House, 1971), p. 2.

166   Noebel, p. 124.

167   "State homicide laws that recognize unborn victims," www.nrlc.org/Unborn_Victims/Statehomicidelaws092302.html (accessed August 2009).

168   McDowell, *The Last Christian Generation*, p. 44.

169   Colson, p. 69.

170   *The Truth Project*.

171   "Unplugging Truth in a Morally Suicidal Culture," http://www.rzim.org/CA/Resources/Listen/JustThinking.aspx?archive=1and pid=1027 (accessed August 2009).

172   McDowell, *The Last Christian Generation*, p. 43.

173   Pearcey, p. 111.

174   Ibid., p. 21.

175   Ibid., p. 35.

176   Ibid., p. 69.

177   Ibid., p. 39.

178   Ibid., p. 116.

179   McDowell, *The Last Christian Generation*, p. 52.

180   Lisa Miller, "We are all Hindus now," *Newsweek*, August 24 and 31, 2009, p. 70.

181   Pearcey, p. 217.

182   McDowell, *The Last Christian Generation*, p. 55.

183   Noebel, p. 122.

184   Pearcey, p. 110.

185   Ibid., p. 119.

186   Ibid., p. 220.

187   Ibid., pp. 119, 121.

188   Ibid., p. 44.

189   Noebel, p. 14.

190   Pearcey, p. 126.

191   Ibid., p. 149.